Books and Magazines

Books and Magazines

A Guide to Publishing and Bookselling Courses in the United States

Published with the Support of the United States Information Agency

Peterson's Guides
Princeton, New Jersey

Library of Congress Cataloging-in-Publication Data

Books and magazines : a guide to publishing and bookselling courses in the
    United States.
       p.   cm.
    Includes index.
    ISBN 1-56079-088-1 (pbk.)
    1. Publishers and publishing—Study and teaching—United States—
Directories. 2. Book industries and trade—Study and teaching—United
States—Directories. 3. Periodicals, Publishing of—Study and teaching—
United States—Directories. 4. Booksellers and bookselling—Study and
teaching—United States—Directories.
I. Peterson's Guides, Inc.
Z285.35.U5B66   1991
381'%45002'07073—dc20   91-41014

Composition and design by Peterson's Guides

Printed in the United States of America

10 9 8 7 6 5 4 3 2 1

Table of Contents

Preface

The United States Information Agency's Book and Library Advisory Committee consists of a group of private citizens—most of whom are book publishing executives and specialists in library science. One of the goals of the committee is to provide guidance and education to publishers in different parts of the world—with special attention to those in Eastern Europe and Third World countries. It became evident that an important step toward that end would be the compilation of a directory to the professional training courses in publishing and bookselling that are available in the United States—and *Books and Magazines* is the result.

It is the hope of the committee that publishers the world over will find this guide a valuable "first stop" reference tool that can help them in a number of ways. For those considering starting their own educational programs, it can provide valuable connections to those who have experience to share in designing and running such courses. Additionally, it provides a rich resource of opportunities for study in America that can fulfill another of USIA's goals—to facilitate the exchange of professional expertise across national borders.

S. William Pattis, Chairman
Book and Library Advisory Committee

Elizabeth A. Geiser, Chairman
Subcommittee on International
    Publishing Education

United States Information Agency

Foreword

The publishing industry in North America has coined the phrase "the accidental profession" to describe how it is that the people who are employed at the various tasks needed to bring writer and reader together came to be doing what they are doing. Bookselling is an integral part of the industry and an exemplar of its accidental nature. The personnel files of bookstores across the country are swollen with the resumes of students who are on their way to a career in something else. And among the ranks of bookstore owners are people who have had other jobs but find bookselling most fulfilling. Becoming a bookseller is often not a first-choice career and is rarely a second choice, which underscores the value of formal training for individuals who find they have become, happily, bookpeople.

While priding itself on being a people business—in which creative ability is valued over trade skills—the publishing industry has been remarkably complacent about recruiting and developing its talent. Today, it can no longer afford the luxury of finding its people by accident or having them accidentally find it. As our culture moves more heavily into service businesses and as the information explosion exponentially increases the need for highly qualified people to staff all businesses, the book industry requires the best of the best. As the nexus between social-, cultural-, and scientific-information producers and consumers, booksellers play an increasingly more important role in society. To help meet that responsibility, bookpeople can learn from the experiences and traditions of the past and the visions of the future expounded by the faculty and speakers of the programs and seminars profiled in this book. I urge you, take advantage of the opportunities presented here.

Bernard E. Rath, Executive Director
American Booksellers Association

Foreword

The magazine industry is an exciting and challenging place to work. The explosion of start-up magazines that occurred in the last decade provided many new employment opportunities for young people entering the job market and for professionals already working in the field. But the ability to take full advantage of the opportunities that exist today requires up-to-date knowledge and a variety of skills—knowledge and skills that even people who have had some basic instruction or experience in journalism, business, or magazine publishing may lack.

Books and Magazines identifies a rich variety of courses and seminars designed to meet the needs of people interested in beginning a career in magazine publishing and of experienced professionals who wish to upgrade their skills or areas of expertise.

Compared to programs that offer instruction in newspaper or book publishing, courses in magazine publishing are relatively new. Driven by the growing demand for better trained professionals, there has been a proliferation of courses and seminars that cover the full range of skills needed in magazine publishing and the issues central to it. Universities, trade associations such as the Magazine Publishers of America, and trade magazines are creating a rich menu of training opportunities open to virtually everyone who is interested.

The magazine business is dynamic. It is constantly being bombarded by changes in reader interest, preferences, and life-styles; changes in print and production technology; and changes in the way advertisers market their products. Its professionals need to quickly absorb and adjust to those changes. And because its marketplace is becoming more competitive, those who don't adopt new and smarter ways to work often get left behind.

I urge anyone who wants to become a magazine professional or who wants to sharpen their on-the-job skills to examine the courses profiled in this book. You are certain to find one or two that fit your particular needs and aspirations. Magazine publishing is a creative and exciting field. And the future of the industry will be shaped by the best-trained and best-qualified individuals.

Donald D. Kummerfeld, President
Magazine Publishers of America

How to Use This Book

Books and Magazines is intended for people who are interested in beginning a career in book publishing, magazine publishing, or bookselling and for those already employed in these fields who wish to increase their professional knowledge. The programs featured in it are offered by leading education institutions and by some of the industry's top professional associations. They offer comprehensive courses of study covering many aspects of publishing or provide detailed instruction in such individual areas as editorial, production, management, sales, graphic arts, or printing.

The profiles were collected during the summer of 1991. Questionnaires were sent to two- and four-year colleges and to professional associations that offer programs meeting the criteria outlined above, and all data were submitted by officials of these programs. The extent of the information and the descriptions of the programs reflect these respondents' points of view. In addition, a majority of the institutions that submitted data were contacted directly by Peterson's editorial staff to verify facts, resolve discrepancies, and obtain additional information. Because of this comprehensive editorial review and because all material comes directly from program officials, we have every reason to believe that the information presented in this guide is accurate. However, prospective students should check with the program contact identified in the listings he or she is interested in to verify such information as tuition and fees, which may have changed since the publication of this book.

The institutions and associations that offer programs are listed alphabetically on the pages that follow. The subjects covered by these programs range from copyediting, writing, and author/editor relations to production to managing a publishing operation. Several programs encompass book buying and/or selling and are targeted for wholesalers, retailers, and bookstore owners and staff. As an added feature, programs in graphic arts and printing are included that offer training and/or insight into the technical skills needed for the various jobs that make up those professions. Subject and geographical indexes have been compiled to help readers identify programs by topics covered and location.

While the content of each profile is unique, the type of information conveyed is standard thoughout. Each begins with the name and location of the institution or association providing the program, followed by the program name, the department or division that sponsors it, and the level it is geared toward (undergraduate, graduate, or professional). Next is a statement of objective. Under a separate heading is a program description that includes course names or topics; the credit or type of degree completion of the program leads to; the number of courses required to complete it; whether classes meet on weekdays, evenings, or weekends; how long students typically take to complete the program; prerequisites (if any); whether it involves field trips, internships, or special projects; and whether job placement services are available. Admission data relays program competitiveness, entry requirements, and the most current enrollment figures available. The profiles also contain faculty listings, program fees, information on housing, and a listing for the program contact.

The development of *Books and Magazines* benefited from the advice of many publishing professionals and organizations. Among those we would especially like to thank are S. William Pattis and Elizabeth A. Geiser of the Book and Library Advisory Committee of the United States Information Agency, Bernard E. Rath and Carol Miles of the American Booksellers Association, Nicholas A. Veliotes and Barbara J. Meredith of the Association of American Publishers, Donald D. Kummerfeld and Russell J. Melvin of the Magazine Publishers of America, and our contributing essayists, Jeremiah Kaplan, Ruth R. Whitney, and Joyce Meskis.

Book Publishing: A Lifetime Education

Jeremiah Kaplan, Director, Scholastic, Inc., and
former Chairman, Macmillan Publishing Company

There was a time when the tools of the trade in book publishing were simple and familiar—pencils, erasers, fountain pens, scissors, adding machines, typewriters, carbon paper, and trunk-telephone operators. Entry-level jobs were viewed as apprenticeships, and there seemed to be endless time for on-the-job learning. But this changed in the 1950s and has been changing ever since. The size and complexity of publishing organizations have grown tremendously and the introduction of new tools and the techniques to use them has been increasingly more rapid. For the most part, on-the-job training is a thing of the past. It is no longer possible to get or keep a job without having some kind of formal, industry-specific training.

The growth of book publishing can be attributed to two major developments: the acquisition of privately owned publishing houses by public corporations and the development of new channels of distribution. First, the public corporations had the capital to turn the private houses into large companies. Second, new distribution methods—large chains, telemarketing, and mail order—increased sales to levels that were previously unheard of. And these developments triggered other changes: Marketing received more emphasis, computer technology was embraced, and employees at all levels (not just accountants) were made aware of the importance of the bottom line.

The list of what people who aspire to work in book publishing or those already working in the field should know about the industry and their profession is long. Among the most important things they should be aware of is that continuous change is an integral part of the business. Being hired for a job or being promoted to management will be the result of mastering the skills needed to stay on top of technological changes and understanding the responsibilities of the other players in the organization as they develop. The future of book publishing belongs to those who recognize this and commit to becoming lifelong students of it.

Books and Magazines is a remarkable resource. I welcome it and am sure that it will become an indispensable directory for those who are interested in mastering the art of book publishing.

Magazine Publishing: Focusing on the Big Picture

Ruth R. Whitney, Editor-in-Chief
Glamour

Magazine publishing in the 1990s presents a changed picture from the boom years of the 1980s. The industry is both hurting and benefiting from the economic downturn. Weekly and monthly magazines alike are zigging and zagging to respond to the current zeitgeist. Publishers may not yet know what this decade is all about, but it is clear that it's nothing like the decade of material excess that preceded it.

The driving force of magazine publishing today is focus—focus not only in niche marketing and sales but also in editorial offices and art departments. Every marketing and sales executive, editor, and art director is looking more seriously and more assiduously than before for the sharpest possible focus for his or her product. These professionals are identifying their strengths and making the most of them, whether that means beefing up coverage of topics that have maximum appeal to readers or spinning off special issues that will be money-makers. The momentum is affecting circulation departments as well. Soft single-copy sales have driven circulation managers to find dependable paths to that elusive, big-selling cover.

The industry has seen an extraordinary amount of redesigning, repositioning, and cover testing going on and an increase in the use of focus groups because there is less room for marketplace trial and error than there once was. This is a time of toughening up and maturation for the industry. In the current climate, the hesitant step, the self-indulgent step, and the uninformed step are all dangerous.

Decision making in publishing can no longer be an isolated process. Marketing, sales, editorial, and circulation affect each other like tumbling dominoes. Today, more than in the past, the ability to understand the broad ramifications of each decision is not just a valuable asset but also a crucial one. This reality requires that individual players master their own jobs and have a solid understanding of the big picture. An educated staff, alert to every breath of change, is the strongest backup an editor or publisher can have. It can make a magazine's larger goals coherent and achievable.

The courses described in *Books and Magazines* offer solid credentials for people looking for a job in a tough market. Moreover, multiple skills and a full understanding of the marketplace are the surest route to promotion.

Bookselling in the 1990s: Turning Challenges into Opportunities

Joyce Meskis, President
American Booksellers Association

In some ways, bookselling in the 1990s is business as usual. The same old issues remain: returns, out-of-stock situations, the mind-boggling logistics of over 27,000 publishers trying to distribute some one million titles in print across a large country and a larger world, the difficulty of getting communications from the field about what's hot and what's not, discounts, co-op policies, collections, and freight. And competition is everywhere—not only among bookstores but in the publishing community as well—for authors, for editors, for reviewers' attention, for shelf space in the store. Bookstores must compete with other industries for customers' discretionary dollars and time. In my home state of Colorado, where the sun shines a lot of the time and the terrain is breathtakingly beautiful, even the weather is a competitor, and booksellers pray for rain to drive people indoors.

But if some things have stayed the same, others have not. The bookstore itself has changed dramatically over the past four decades. In the 1950s, trade books were found primarily in small bookshops that had an image of being for intellectuals only. Trendier fare was found in the book department of the department store or on a rack in the corner drugstore. Today, by way of contrast, there are more creative ways and a greater variety of formats for bringing books to the attention of the public than ever before. Ranging from the traditional mom-and-pop store to the logistically sophisticated chain operation, from the local hardware store offering books on home improvement to the warehouse selling stacks of a limited but highly discounted selection of books alongside its other merchandise, each format represents its own brand of bookselling, and each makes its own contribution to the effort to develop a wider and deeper readership.

The past two decades in particular have witnessed many changes in the bookselling environment. The large, independent, regional store has come of age, with its approximately 100,000 titles and special services to the customer. And, with the coming of the chains to the high-traffic shopping mall, the bookstore has been positioned in the mainstream of American life, offering some 10,000 titles and a more or less self-service approach.

With their deep pockets, savvy buying, and aggressive marketing policies, the new chains placed added competitive pressures on the traditional chains and independent operators. Over the past decade, the response of the traditional chains was to reposition themselves with broader, deeper discounting of books and the increased provision of more profitable nonbook products, while the independents increasingly professionalized their operations. Specialty stores became more prevalent, especially in the area of children's books, and the general stores increased their inventories and offered more services. The reading public responded favorably and increased its support of local independents, with the result that, in pockets around the country, some independent stores grew to 50,000 square feet and offered more than 150,000 titles.

These developments, combined with a decline in the construction of shopping malls and increasing price competition, pushed the chains into a further repositioning. Small chains were absorbed into larger ones, and the marketing mix shifted to offer broader inventories, more services, and such special promotions as "preferred reader" programs to encourage repeat sales. The chains began opening much larger stores—the day of the superstore had come. And so had bookselling from abroad, as Waterstone's, the British bookselling phenomenon, crossed the Atlantic to open a 25,000-square-foot shop in the heart of Boston, the first of its planned stores in a number of U.S. cities.

One of the challenges to booksellers in the current climate is how to maintain a healthy balance among the chain, chain discount, and independent stores, not to mention the book clubs and direct-mail sellers. This will necessitate broadening the readership base so that publishers can divide their efforts between bringing out new books and keeping titles in print, ensuring a diversity that can support independents large and small as well as the chains. The chains' earlier efforts have shown that the readership base can indeed be broadened, and the independent stores seem to have succeeded in creating an interest in areas in which there has formerly been little. Each has created its own sphere of good bookselling, enticing the reader and supporting the varied efforts of the publishing industry.

So, while sellers naturally respond in some measure to customers' needs and interests, the real excitement for booksellers in the Nineties will be in anticipating and creating new needs and interests. They will have to pique the curiosity of potential readers, reaching out in ways that strengthen individual businesses and, more importantly, cement the foundation of a reading society.

What will it take to get the job done? Of course, successful booksellers must combine their passion for bringing books to the people with an awareness of the bottom line. They will know the traits of both existing and potential customers. They will have detailed knowledge of what is being published and present customers with a sampling sufficient to entice but not so great as to threaten the financial stability of the store. The selection will be displayed in an appealing manner, accompanied by impeccable service.

In other words, the best booksellers will be skilled in the art of making the customer's trip to the bookstore a memorable and pleasant experience. The creation of that experience will have to include such things as merchandising to the occasional passerby as well as the serious browser, service in excess of expectations, and an element of surprise at every turn within an essentially restful setting. And the bookstore needs to become known as *the place* to buy books, the house of ideas, a community resource. In fact, one of the bookseller's most challenging tasks for this decade is getting the public to recognize and support this concept.

To illustrate, a New Mexico bookseller has been setting up book tables at meetings of community organizations in rural areas that have no bookstores. "There is a tremendous hunger for books here," he said. "One such table . . . sold seventy-three books to a gathering of thirty people, with *every one* of those thirty people buying at least one book!" To sell $627-worth of books, he had traveled 250 miles each way and expended 16 hours' labor plus travel costs. Many would argue that he should cut back on such unprofitable activities, but he was taking advantage of a unique opportunity to expand the potential market, one of the most important things a contemporary bookseller can be doing. Granted, the energy, staffing, and dollars it takes are enormous. The effort is labor- and expense-intensive, but the cost is justified in terms of the ultimate benefit to the industry as a whole.

Of course, this expansion can't be brought about by booksellers acting alone or in a vacuum. Who should bear the brunt of the cost of development? How should the responsibility be shared? And who will regulate the forces of competition that, unregulated, could sap the resources necessary for such expansion? Who will ensure that booksellers are actually *enhancing* and *expanding* the market rather than just jockeying for market share? Who will see that bookstores do business in an equitable manner, attentive to the needs of a highly diverse reading public without reacting to each passing whim? The answer? It falls to each bookseller, of whatever type, to watch over the balance of factors that will build a reading society today for the future of the industry.

There are good tools with which to work—sound regional booksellers associations and, in the American Booksellers Association (ABA), a strong national organization. To help booksellers become more professional—and profitable—ABA offers a variety of educational programs and services. The Booksellers Schools, now in their twenty-fifth year, are taught by volunteer professionals working in the book trade: bookstore owners, managers, and publishing personnel. There are schools for all levels of bookselling experience, from prospective to advanced professional, and for the special needs of children's booksellers and the staff of large stores. Panels and roundtables at the annual ABA convention and one-day seminars held throughout the country by the ABA and the regional associations address specific concerns of booksellers. A new videotape lending library offers ABA members professionally produced programs on staff management, customer service, time management, and other business issues, as well as on such specialized topics as children's bookselling and the computerization of the retail bookstore.

The tools are there. The opportunities are there. Some of the choices along the way may be hard ones to make, but it is important for booksellers to take the long view in the interests of building an industry and a readership ready for the next century.

Profiles of Publishing and Bookselling Courses in the United States

About Books, Inc.
Buena Vista, Colorado

BOOK PUBLISHING SUCCESS STRATEGIES/BOOK PROMOTION AND MARKETING SECRETS

Level
Undergraduate/Professional

Program Objective
Designed to inform writers, professionals, entrepreneurs, and independent small publishers about how to produce quality product and successfully market it nationwide.

Program Description
Two single seminars. Seminars meet weekdays, evenings, weekends and run one to two days. Job placement not available.

Book Publishing Success Strategies examines the ways to get books into print, focusing on trade and self-publishing. Topics include business aspects, developing product, and marketing strategies.

Book Promotion and Marketing Secrets examines how to tap into free public relations, traditional trade channels of distribution, and special sales outlets. Topics include advertising, direct mail, and writing promotional materials.

Admission
Admission open. Requires registration.

Faculty
Marilyn Ross, vice president, About Books, Inc.; Tom Ross, president, About Books, Inc.

Expenses and Accommodations
$59–$195 per course. $4–$8 application fee. Housing not available.

Contact   Suzanne Miller, Coordinator
P.O. Box 1500-B
Buena Vista, CO 81211
719-395-2459; fax 719-395-8374

American Booksellers Association
New York, New York

ABA ADVANCED BUSINESS MANAGEMENT SCHOOL

Sponsor
Department of Professional Development and Education

Level
Professional

Program Objective
Designed to help experienced owners and managers enhance their understanding of current management principles by exposing them to sound, up-to-date business practices in the context of real management situations.

Program Description
Participative lectures, case-study discussions, small-group work, and experimental exercises cover such subjects as financial analysis and management, market opportunity analysis, asset management, strategic plan development, employee relations and motivation, and financial forecasting and growth. Completion of the five-day program results in a certificate. Program held weekdays, evenings, weekends. Job placement services not available.

Admission
Admission selective. Registration limited to 36 individuals with experience in the book industry. Requires application.

Faculty
Faculty is composed of experienced professionals who work in the book trade: bookstore owners, bookstore managers, and publishing personnel.

Expenses and Accommodations
$400–$600 for the entire program. Housing available.

Contact   Coordinator
ABA Booksellers Schools
American Booksellers Association
137 West 25th Street, 11th Floor
New York, NY 10001-7296
212-463-8450 Ext. 203; fax 212-463-9359

American Booksellers Association
New York, New York

ABA BASIC PROFESSIONAL BOOKSELLERS SCHOOL

Sponsor
Department of Professional Development and Education

Level
Professional

Program Objective
Designed for individuals from stores that have been in business for less than two years that have grossed less than $250,000. The program is scheduled to meet just before the ABA Convention to provide students with the opportunity to combine classroom experience with the opportunity to buy inventory.

Program Description
Presentations, group projects, and interactive training methods cover such subjects as financial planning and management, store layout and display, inventory management and buying books, staff management, customer service and retail selling, promotion and publicity, marketing and advertising principles, expanding a market, and the publishing process. Elective sessions on special interest topics are also held. Completion of the four-day program results in a certificate. Program held weekdays, evenings, weekends. Job placement services not available.

Admission
Admission selective. Registration limited to 75 individuals from bookstores that have been in business less than two years and grossed less than $250,000. Requires application.

Faculty
Faculty is composed of experienced professionals who work in the book trade: bookstore owners, bookstore managers, and publishing personnel.

Expenses and Accommodations
$400–$600 for the entire program. Housing available.

Contact   Coordinator
ABA Booksellers Schools
American Booksellers Association
137 West 25th Street, 11th Floor
New York, NY 10001-7296
212-463-8450 Ext. 203; fax 212-463-9359

American Booksellers Association
New York, New York

ABA CHILDREN'S BOOKSELLERS SCHOOL

Sponsor
Department of Professional Development and Education

Level
Professional

Program Objective
Designed for experienced, professional bookstore owners and staff currently engaged in the retail sale of children's trade books who want to improve their profitability and service to the community.

Program Description
Presentations, group projects, and interactive training methods cover the same subjects as the ABA Professional Booksellers School profiled on the preceding page plus current issues in children's bookselling. Elective sessions on special interest topics (e.g., in-store events with or without authors, becoming a community resource center, selling trade books to schools, out-of-store sales, and newsletters). Completion of the four-day program results in a certificate. Program held weekdays, evenings, weekends. Job placement services not available.

Admission
Admission selective. Registration limited to 55 experienced bookstore owners or staff members who are currently engaged in the retail sale of children's trade books. Requires application.

Faculty
Faculty is composed of experienced professionals who work in the book trade: bookstore owners, bookstore managers, and publishing personnel.

Expenses and Accommodations
$400–$600 for the entire program. Housing available.

Contact   Coordinator
ABA Booksellers Schools
American Booksellers Association
137 West 25th Street, 11th Floor
New York, NY 10001-7296
212-463-8450 Ext. 203; fax 212-463-9359

American Booksellers Association
New York, New York

ABA LARGE STORE STAFF SCHOOL

Sponsor
Department of Professional Development and Education

Level
Professional

Program Objective
Designed for the staff of large bookstores with managers who are looking for sophisticated solutions to the problems associated with running a store with gross sales over $1-million.

Program Description
Presentations, group projects, and interactive training methods explore business principles associated with fast growth and accelerated profitability, including such topics as employee relations and in-store communications, buying strategies and inventory budgeting, customer relations, personnel management, financial concepts, the publishing process, and developing organizational models. Completion of the four-day program results in a certificate. Program held weekdays, evenings, weekends. Job placement services not available.

Admission
Admission selective. Registration limited to 75 staff members of stores with gross sales over $1-million. Requires application.

Faculty
Faculty is composed of experienced professionals who work in the book trade: bookstore owners, bookstore managers, and publishing personnel.

Expenses and Accommodations
$400–$600 for the entire program. Housing available.

Contact   Coordinator
ABA Booksellers Schools
American Booksellers Association
137 West 25th Street, 11th Floor
New York, NY 10001-7296
212-463-8450 Ext. 203; fax 212-463-9359

American Booksellers Association
New York, New York

ABA PROFESSIONAL BOOKSELLERS SCHOOL

Sponsor
Department of Professional Development and Education

Level
Professional

Program Objective
Designed for those who have several years of hands-on experience working in a bookstore—owners, managers, and staff—and others in the book industry who want to know more about bookselling.

Program Description
Presentations, group projects, and interactive training methods cover such subjects as financial planning and management, store layout and display, inventory management and buying books, staff management, customer service and retail selling, promotion and publicity, marketing and advertising principles, expanding a market, and the publishing process. Elective sessions on special interest topics are also held. Completion of the four-day program results in a certificate. Program held weekdays, evenings, weekends. Job placement services not available.

Admission
Admission selective. Registration limited to 75 individuals with experience in the book industry. Requires application.

Faculty
Faculty is composed of experienced professionals who work in the book trade: bookstore owners, bookstore managers, and publishing personnel.

Expenses and Accommodations
$400–$600 for the entire program. Housing available.

Contact   Coordinator
ABA Booksellers Schools
American Booksellers Association
137 West 25th Street, 11th Floor
New York, NY 10001-7296
212-463-8450 Ext. 203; fax 212-463-9359

American Booksellers Association
New York, New York

ABA PROSPECTIVE BOOKSELLERS SCHOOL

Sponsor
Department of Professional Development and Education

Level
Professional

Program Objective
Designed for those in the process of opening a store for the first time or those who are seriously considering the possibility of opening one.

Program Description
Presentations, group projects, and interactive training methods cover such subjects as financial realities, site selection and lease negotiation, physical planning and store layout, financial planning and management, initial inventory selection, ordering and receiving procedures, physical inventory management, computers in the bookstore, store and staff management, merchandising and display, and advertising and promotion. Also included are advisory sessions to answer individual needs and elective sessions on special interest topics (e.g., children's books, nonbook sales, and out-of-store sales). Completion of the four-day program results in a certificate. Program held weekdays, evenings, weekends. Job placement services not available.

Admission
Admission selective. Registration limited to 75. Requires application.

Faculty
Faculty is composed of experienced professionals who work in the book trade: bookstore owners, bookstore managers, and publishing personnel.

Expenses and Accommodations
$400–$600 for the entire program. Housing available.

Contact   Coordinator
ABA Booksellers Schools
American Booksellers Association
137 West 25th Street, 11th Floor
New York, NY 10001-7296
212-463-8450 Ext. 203; fax 212-463-9353

Arkansas State University
Jonesboro, Arkansas

PRINTING

Sponsor
Department of Journalism and Printing

Level
Undergraduate

Program Objective
To prepare men and women for careers in printing.

Program Description
Courses include Basic Printing Practices, Phototypesetting, Small Offset Presses, Bindery and Finishing Operations, Copy Preparation and Paste-up, Paper and Ink, Graphic Arts Film Procedures, Image Assembly for Platemaking, Estimating I, Estimating II, Management of Printing Production, Color Reproduction, Offset Presses, Practicum in Printing, Screen Process Printing, Desktop Publishing and Design, Current Printing Practices, Printing Internship, and Special Problems in Printing. Thirteen courses are needed to complete the program, which leads to a bachelor's degree; students typically take courses over eight semesters. Classes meet weekdays. Includes internships and special projects. Job placement services available.

Admission
Admission open to students enrolled at the university. In the academic year 1990–91, 12 applied, 10 were accepted, 8 enrolled.

Faculty
Bob Kern, director of printing; Pat Tinnin, instructor of printing.

Expenses and Accommodation
$1,400 tuition per year (state residents); $12,650 (nonresidents). $1,095–$1,220 per semester for room and board.

Contact   Joel Gambill, Chairman
Department of Journalism and Printing
P.O. Box 1930
Jonesboro, AR 72467
501-972-3075; fax 501-972-3858

Association of American Publishers
New York, New York

INTERNATIONAL SEMINARS

Sponsor
International Professional Development Committee

Level
Professional

Program Objective
Designed to provide education and training for publishing professionals in editing, rights, international sales and marketing, contracts, and literary agencies.

Program Description
Recent seminar topics included Buying a Book: Are You Getting Enough for Your Company's Money?, Publishing and Bookselling Around the World, and Protecting Your Overseas Markets. Seminars end with a question-and-answer period. Seminars meet weekdays for whole- or half-day sessions. Job placement services not available.

Admission
Admission open on a space-available basis. Total enrollment for the 1990 seminars was 250. Application required.

Faculty
Speakers vary from seminar to seminar and are usually from the international publishing arena.

Expenses and Accommodations
Expenses N/A (member and nonmember rates). Housing not available.

Contact   Barbara Meredith, Director
International Division
Association of American Publishers
220 East 23rd Street
New York, NY 10010
212-689-8920; fax 212-696-0131

Association of American Publishers
New York, New York

PROFESSIONAL AND SCHOLARLY SEMINARS

Sponsor
Professional Scholarly Publishing Journals and/or PSP Marketing Committee

Level
Professional

Program Objective
Designed to educate and train publishers in the academic, journal, and professional publications fields.

Program Description
Recent seminar topics included Orientation to Professional Scholarly Marketing and Journal Management Workshop. Seminars end with a question-and-answer period. Seminars meet in whole- or half-day sessions. Job placement services not available.

Admission
Admission open on a space-available basis. Total enrollment for the 1990 seminars was 200. Application required.

Faculty
Speakers vary from seminar to seminar.

Expenses and Accommodations
Expenses N/A (member and nonmember rates). Housing not available.

Contact   Barbara Meredith, Director
Professional Scholarly Publishing
Association of American Publishers
220 East 23rd Street
New York, NY 10010
212-689-8920; fax 212-696-0131

Association of American University Presses
New York, New York

AAUP WORKSHOPS

Level
Professional

Program Objective
AAUP programs are designed to help its member presses market their publications and train their personnel more effectively than they could do on their own.

Program Description
Each year the AAUP sponsors several workshops on a variety of subjects. Recent topics included journal management, finances for nonfinancial people, jacket design, electronic publishing, fund-raising, acquisitions, and photography for the university press editor. Workshops held weekdays; evening reception. Workshops typically last two to three days. Students sometimes required to do reading assignments in advance. Job placement services not available.

Admission
Admission open (AAUP members have priority). Enrollment limited to between 25 and 50 per workshop. Requires registration.

Faculty
Faculty composed of professionals in the field.

Expenses and Accommodations
$60–$200 per workshop (includes course materials and meals). Housing available.

Contact   Hollis Holmes, Assistant Executive Director
Association of American University Presses
584 Broadway
Suite 410
New York, NY 10012
212-941-6610

Association of the Graphic Arts
New York, New York

EVENING SCHOOL GRAPHIC ARTS CAREER ADVANCEMENT PROGRAM

Sponsor
Education and Training

Level
Professional

Program Objective
Designed to provide programs for career advancement and training and development opportunities for new entrants in the graphic arts industry. Targeted graphic arts professionals include printers, designers, finishers, sales and marketing personnel, estimators, strippers, and managers.

Program Description
Courses include Desktop Publishing, Introduction to Printing, How to Buy Print, Typography for the '90s, Paper for the Graphic Arts, Color Separation, Advanced Print Production, Direct Mail Production, Prepress Technology, Successful Catalog Design, Quality Control, Managing Through a Recession, How to Be a Better Manager, Sales Success, Developing Marketing Strategy, Customer Service, Estimating I and II, Production for Designers, Color Lithography, Offset Lithography, Personalization, Design, Preparing Artwork That Works, Credit and Collections, Postscript, and Public Relations. Program awards Certificate of Achievement (120 hours), Certificate of Graphic Arts Study (240 hours), and Certified Printing Executive (240 hours). Six to eighteen courses are required for certificate. Courses meet weekdays, evenings, weekends and run for ten weeks (20 hours). Includes field trips and special projects. Job placement services available.

Admission
Admission open. In 1990, 700 applied, 700 were accepted, 700 enrolled. One to three years of previous experience in publishing is recommended for some courses.

Faculty
John L. Aaron, account executive/production coordinator, Kwik International Color, Ltd.; David Azar, Hudson Printing Co.; Paul Baim, Huxley Envelope Company; Alan Barnett, production manager, Tanagraphics, Inc.; John Basmagy, Majestic Packaging Co.; John R. Battiloro, graphic arts consultant; Annette Wolf Bensen, sales executive, Expertype, Inc.; Michael Bevacqua, Castlereagh Press; Linda Bistany, sales, Moore Response Marketing; Peter Burmeister, senior vice president—corporate, Drucker Printing Co.; Ellen Bush, Ammirati & Puris, Inc.; Michele Duffy, production supervisor, Book-of-the-Month Club; Arnold Egeland, estimator and production manager, Case-Hoyt Printers; Meg Feeley, estimator, Seybert-Nicholas; David Friedman, CPC Reprographics, Inc.; Robert J. Gardella, senior purchasing agent, Hoffman–La Roche; Richard Goldberg, E&B Marine, Inc.; Sal Guadagna, DJS Business Systems; Bob Hansen, creative art director, Cableview Publications; Adolph Hendler, graphic arts management consultant; Michael Karp, president, Don Aux Associates, Inc.; Ed Khaleel, president, Khaleel Associates; Thomas V. Kinney, president, TK Consulting; Jack Letizia, Applied Graphics Technologies; George Luthcke Jr., print production coordinator, Panorama Press; Jane I. Madson, In-House Publishing; Kenneth Margolies, technical training manager, Hoechst Celanese, Enco Printing Products Division; Paul Marinelli, art director/senior computer designer and illustrator, Gianettino & Meredith Advertis-

ing; Don Merit, graphic arts consultant; Roderick Miller, technology teacher, East Islip Schools; Andy Perni Jr., president, Design Art, Ltd.; Margaret Peters, partner, Peters & Feldman Marketing Communications; Sal Pinzone, offset pressman, Impressions by Harbor View, Ltd.; David Pixley, MicroTrek; Joanne Reddan, Design on Disk, Inc.; Gary Ritkes, technical account executive, Applied Graphics Technologies; Thomas Saggiomo, business manager, Hoechst Celanese, Printing Products Division; Joseph Salpeter, production, The Trident Group; Michael Schneider, MicroTrek; Sid Snyder, retired assistant principal—supervision and chairman of the Related Technology Department of the High School of Graphic and Communication Arts; Thomas A. Stenklyft, executive consultant, I. C. System; Peter A. Vollmuth, MicroTrek; and William Weiss, sales representative, Bulkley Dunton.

Expenses and Accommodations
$150–$450 per course. $15 registration fee. Other expenses include books and field trips. Housing not available.

Contact   Linda E. Nahum, Director, Education and Training
            or Angela Yarkovsky, Registrar
          Evening School
          Association of the Graphic Arts
          5 Penn Plaza
          20th Floor
          New York, NY 10001
          212-279-2111; fax 212-279-5381

Bob Jones University
Greenville, South Carolina

PUBLISHING

Sponsor
Department of Professional Writing and Publication

Level
Undergraduate

Program Objective
To acquaint students with and provide experiences in all phases of present-day book production. The program is for undergraduates interested in a position in a publishing house or working in Christian ministry publications.

Program Description
Courses include Principles of Communication, Fundamentals of Publishing, Expository Writing, Creative or Business Writing, Copy Editing, Public Relations, Graphics, Publishing Internship with Bob Jones University Press, Critical Writing, and Writing Seminar. Program leads to a B.A. in publishing. Degree requires 130 credit hours, 31 of which must be in the student's major. Classes meet daytime. Students typically take courses over eight semesters. Includes internship, field trips, and special projects. Job placement services available.

Admission
Admission is open to students enrolled at the university. Program enrollment figures N/A.

Faculty
Ronald A. Horton, chair, Department of Professional Writing and Publications; Raymond A. St. John, chair, Department of English; George Collins, director of production, Bob Jones University Press.

Expenses and Accommodations
$1,830 tuition per semester. $25 application fee. $45 graduation fee. Housing available.

Contact   David Christ, Director of Admissions
Bob Jones University
Greenville, SC 29614
803-242-5100 Ext. 2050

Bookbinders Guild of New York
New York, New York

FUNDAMENTALS OF BOOK PUBLISHING SEMINAR (FALL)/ADVANCED SEMINAR (SPRING)

Sponsor
Education Committee

Level
Professional

Program Description
The Fundamentals of Book Publishing seminar is designed to give an overview of the book from manuscript to distribution for people who are new to the industry or for those already working in it who want to expand their knowledge. The topic of the advanced seminar varies from year to year and is targeted for professionals with three or more years of experience. Fall seminar meets for three to four half-day sessions, spring seminar for a full-day session. Both meet weekdays. Housing not available.

Admission
Admission open. In 1991, 75 applied, 75 were accepted, 75 enrolled.

Faculty
Speakers vary from year to year.

Expenses and Accommodations
$95–$125 fall series; $75–$125 spring program. Housing not available.

Contact   Michael Wettstein
Bookbinders Guild
c/o Lehigh Press
21 Stuyvesant Street
New York, New York 10003
212-490-8700

Bookbuilders of Boston
Woburn, Massachusetts

FALL ROUNDTABLE SEMINARS/ADVANCED SEMINARS

Level
Professional

Program Objective
Designed as a forum where members of the publishing community can learn fundamentals and be kept informed about new trends.

Program Description
The Fall Roundtable consists of seven 2-hour evening seminars (though the number may vary from year to year) plus a field trip. This year the topics include career path alternatives in the changing marketplace; electronic design; perfecting color separations; identifying markets for free-lance skills; and explanations of multimedia, educational technology, and interactive learning systems. The advanced seminars are a series of one-day sessions designed for publishing professionals with a working knowledge of most aspects of publishing. Individuals may sign up for as many seminars as they wish; seminars meet daytime and evenings. Includes field trips. Job placement not available.

Admission
Admission open (including nonmembers and students).

Faculty
Speakers change from year to year.

Expenses and Accommodations
Fall Roundtable per seminar fee—$15 for members, $20 for nonmembers, and $10 for students. Field trip fee. Advanced Seminars per seminar—$40 for members, $50 nonmembers, and $20 students.

Contact   Sharon Grant, President
Bookbuilders of Boston
112 Cummings Park
Woburn, MA 01801
617-933-6878; fax 617-935-0132

Boston University
Boston, Massachusetts

MAGAZINE WRITING AND PUBLISHING

Sponsor
Department of Journalism, College of Communication

Level
Undergraduate

Course Objective
The course is designed to instruct students in the basic skills they will need for a career in magazine or desktop publishing. Instruction ranges from writing to producing camera-ready pages.

Course Description
Each semester, students write and produce two magazines. The hands-on course is taught in the Macintosh lab, which has PageMaker capability. Each terminal is equipped with up-to-date software. Students are instructed in layout design, copyediting, feature writing, and production. The course runs for one semester and is offered for four credits. Classes meet weekdays. Includes special projects. Job placement services available.

Admission
Admission open to matriculated students on a first-come, first-served basis. Also accepts non-degree students. Enrollment limited to 20. Required for students in magazine sequence. Proficiency with Microsoft Word software is recommended.

Faculty
Caryl Rivers, professor, Department of Journalism, and author; Mitchell Hays, lecturer, Department of Journalism, and designer, *Lowell Sun.*

Expenses and Accommodations
$15,950 tuition per year (full-time students). $45 application fee (full-time students). Course requires $25 lab fee. Housing available.

Contact   Geri Stanton, Secretary
Department of Journalism
Boston University
640 Commonwealth Avenue
Boston, MA 02215
617-353-3484

California Polytechnic State University
San Luis Obispo, California

GRAPHIC COMMUNICATION

Sponsor
Graphic Communication Department

Level
Undergraduate

Program Objective
Designed to prepare students for careers in the graphic arts, with concentrations in computer graphic communication, printing technology, design reproduction technology, and printing management. The computer graphic concentration is for students who want to work with computer applications in the graphic arts. The objective of the printing technology concentration is to assist technically oriented students in understanding the scientific principles that form the basis of the materials, equipment, and processes of printing. In the design reproduction technology concentration, the goal is for students to integrate knowledge of printing technology with principles of design. The objective of the printing management concentration is to offer students a broad foundation of knowledge and problem-solving skills to fill the personnel needs of the printing industry.

Program Description
Courses include Introduction to Graphic Communication, Typography, Introduction to Printing Management, Copy Preparation, Graphic Arts Photography, Electronic Composition Systems, Substrates and Ink, Finishing Processes, Image Assembly/Platemaking, Screen Printing Technology, Print Marketing and Sales, Estimating, Color Image Assembly, Sheetfed Lithographic Technology, Web Printing Technology, Advance Web Printing Technology, Printing Management, Consumer Packaging, Research Methods in Graphic Communication, and a senior project. Program leads to a bachelor's degree. Classes meet weekdays, evenings; students take sixteen quarters to complete course work. Includes field trips, internships, and special projects. Job placement services available.

Computer graphic communication concentration includes the following courses: Fortran Programming, Fundamentals of Computer Science, BASIC Programming, Logic and Switching Circuits, New Technologies in GRC, Computer Principles and Programming, Computer Graphics Applications, C and UNIX, Color Reproduction Control, Estimating/Pricing/Costing, and Computer Imaging.

Design reproduction technology concentration includes 2-D Design Fundamentals, Beginning Color Theory, Color and Design, Pre-Separated Art for Camera, Line and Halftone Media, Typographic Design, Symbology, Corporate Identity, Modern Copy Technology, Advanced Line and Halftone Media, and Advanced Copy Technology.

Printing management concentration includes New Technologies in GRC, Color Reproduction Control, Plant Layout Analysis, Financial Accounting, any 100- or 200-level course, Elements of Marketing, Printing Equipment Management, Printing Management, and Business Law Survey.

Printing technology concentration includes Physics or Chemistry, Technical Calculus, Fortran Programming, New Technologies in GRC, Printing Equipment Management, Color Reproduction Control, Plant Analysis and Design, Computer Imaging, and Analytical Methods for Print.

Admission
Admission is open to all matriculated students. In the 1990–91 academic year 110 students applied, 50 were accepted, 45 enrolled. Requires enrollment at the University.

Faculty
Herschel L. Apfelberg, professor; Michael L. Blum, professor; Gary G. Field, professor; Henry J. Heesch, associate professor; James R. Hutchinson, professor; Harvey R. Levenson, department head; Stephen W. Mott, professor; Patrick A. Munroe, professor; and Philip K. Ruggles, professor.

Expenses and Accommodations
$397 in fees per quarter (state residents); $164 tuition per unit in addition to the per-quarter fees (nonresidents). Housing available.

Contact   Harvey R. Levenson, Department Head
Graphic Communication Department
California Polytechnic State University
San Luis Obispo, CA 93407
805-756-1108; fax 805-756-7118

Carnegie Mellon University
Pittsburgh, Pennsylvania

EDITING AND PUBLISHING

Sponsor
Department of English

Level
Undergraduate/Graduate

Course Objective
The course is designed for people who want experience in all aspects of university press publishing, including selecting manuscripts, copyediting, production, design, advertising, and marketing. Program centers on having each student make a book and being involved in all phases of its production.

Course Description
Topics include manuscript selection, book production, and marketing. Class meets for 50 minutes, three times a week; runs for one semester. Students may need to take it for a second semester to finish their projects. Job placement services available.

Admission
Admission selective. Requires interview with course professor. Open to matriculated undergraduate students and nonmatriculated students. In the academic year 1990–91, 15 applied, 7 were accepted, 7 enrolled.

Faculty
Gerald Costanzo, director, University Press, and professor, Department of English.

Expenses and Accommodations
$15,250 tuition per year. $5,110 room and board. Housing available.

Contact   Gerald Costanzo, Director
University Press
Department of English
Carnegie Mellon University
Pittsburgh, PA 15213-3890
412-268-2861 or 412-268-6348

College of the Ozarks
Point Lookout, Missouri

GRAPHIC ARTS

Sponsor
Graphic Arts Department

Level
Undergraduate

Program Objective
Designed to provide students with a foundation in the technical and managerial knowledge needed for a career in offset lithography.

Program Description
Courses include Introduction to Graphic Arts, Offset Lithography, Typography, Proofreading, Image Generation, Copy Preparation, Offset Presswork, Photomechanical Processes, Production Management, Process Color Separation, and Printing Estimating. Completion of the program leads to a B.S. or B.A. Requires completion of eleven courses. Classes meet weekdays; students usually take eight semesters to complete program. Includes but does not require internships and field trips. Job placement services available.

Admission
Admission open to all matriculated students. In the academic year 1990–91, 25 applied, 25 were accepted, 25 enrolled.

Faculty
Victor Ingrum, associate professor of graphic arts; Jerry Watson, associate professor of graphic arts.

Expenses and Accommodations
$1,700 tuition per year. $500 for books and incidental fees. Housing available.

Contact   Dr. Glen Cameron
Dean of Admissions
College of the Ozarks
Point Lookout, MO 65726
417-334-6411; fax 417-335-2618

College of William and Mary
Williamsburg, Virginia

APPRENTICESHIP AND INTERNSHIP IN EDITING OF HISTORICAL BOOKS AND MAGAZINES

Sponsor
Department of History

Level
Graduate

Program Objective
To provide first-year apprentices with formal instruction in editorial methods and experience in copyediting, proofreading, and other phases of historical publication. To provide second-year interns with on-the-job experience as editorial associates at the Institute for Early American History and Culture, a research institute and publisher of historical monographs and the *William and Mary Quarterly*.

Program Description
Academic courses, professional seminar, and on-the-job training. Program awards M.A. or Ph.D. in American history. Requires completion of 24 or 48 credits. Classes meet weekdays. Students pursuing a master's degree typically complete the program in two semesters; those pursuing a doctorate typically take ten semesters. Includes internship. Job placement services available.

Admission
Admission selective. In the academic year 1990–91, 25 applied, 4 were accepted, 4 enrolled. Requires application, letters of reference, college transcript, undergraduate degree, the aptitude and advanced history tests of the Graduate Record Examination. Interview recommended.

Faculty
Michael McGiffert, Ph.D., professor of history and editor of the *William and Mary Quarterly;* Fredricka Teute, Ph.D., history lecturer and publications editor.

Expenses and Accommodations
$120 per semester credit (state residents); $320 per semester credit (nonresidents). $20 application fee. Housing available.

Contact John Selby, Graduate Director
Department of History
College of William and Mary
Williamsburg, VA 23185
804-221-3720; fax 804-221-2988

College of William and Mary
Williamsburg, Virginia

FERGUSON SEMINAR

Sponsor
Ferguson Endowment

Level
Undergraduate

Program Objective
To familiarize students with the publication industry.

Program Description
Courses include Publishing as a Career in the '90s, Overview of Publishing, Publishing Institutional Books, Publishing Children's Books, Publishing Trade Books, Book Design and Production, and Marketing and Publicizing Books. Requires completion of all courses. Courses meet over two-day seminar. Job placement services available.

Admission
Admission selective and limited to matriculated students. In the 1990–91 academic year, 72 applied, 65 were accepted, 65 enrolled. Requires application, essay.

Faculty
Ron Chambers, editor-in-chief, Praeger Publishers; Betty Prashker, vice president, Crown Publishers; Paul McCarthy, senior editor, Simon & Schuster; Joyce Kachergis, owner, Kachergis Book Design; Daniel Harvey, associate publisher, G. P. Putnam's Sons; Catherine Rigby, editorial associate, Harper Collins Publishers; and Laura Jones Dooley, editor, Yale University Press.

Expenses and Accommodations
$3,396 per year tuition (state residents), $105 per credit hour; $9,246 per year tuition (nonresidents), $280 per credit hour. $5 seminar application fee. Housing available.

Contact   Stanley E. Brown
Director of Career Services
College of William and Mary
Williamsburg, VA 23185
804-221-3240

COSMEP: The International Association of Independent Publishers
San Francisco, California

COSMEP ANNUAL PUBLISHERS' CONFERENCE

Level
Professional

Program Objective
Designed to provide people working in the publishing field with professional expertise in management and book marketing.

Program Description
Topics of the three- to four-day conference change every year. Job placement services not available.

Admission
Admission open. In 1990, 230 attended.

Faculty
Speakers vary from year to year.

Expenses and Accommodations
$175 per conference. $60 membership fee. Housing available.

Contact   Richard Morris, Executive Director
COSMEP
P.O. Box 420703
San Francisco, CA 94142-0703
415-922-9490

Cowles Business Media
Stamford, Connecticut

FOLIO: SHOW (FALL AND SPRING)/MAGAZINE PUBLISHING WEEK (SPRING)

Sponsor
Folio: Conference Division

Level
Professional

Program Objective
Classes are designed for professionals in the magazine industry—beginners and seasoned executives—but students who are interested in learning from publishing practitioners may also attend.

Program Description
Folio: Show is a five-day program of comprehensive training. Courses include The Basics of Magazine Circulation, Starting a New Magazine, A Four-Point Approach to Winning Design, Effective Management of Your Publishing Operation, and The Craft of Interviewing. Magazine Publishing Week refers to regional programs offered in Los Angeles, Chicago, and Washington that are similar in format to the annual Folio: Show but run for two to three days. Classes are held weekdays; some involve advance assignments. Job placement not available.

Admission
Admission open. Total attendance in 1990 was 4,500.

Faculty
Faculty varies from year to year.

Expenses and Accommodations
$95 per 2-hour class. $20 application fee. Housing available.

Contact   Registration Manager
Folio: Show (or *Magazine Publishing Week*)
Box 4232
Stamford, CT 06907-0232
203-358-9900 Ext. 4; fax 203-961-8399

Edinboro University of Pennsylvania
Edinboro, Pennsylvania

BACHELOR OF FINE ARTS

Sponsor
Art Department

Level
Undergraduate

Program Objective
Students acquire the skills needed for careers in printmaking, papermaking, and book arts.

Program Description
Courses include papermaking; book arts; printmaking; lithography; intaglio; relief; screen printing; photolithography; and communications graphics I, II, intermediate, and advanced. Completion of these courses leads to a bachelor's degree. Courses meet weekdays, evenings; students typically take eight semesters to complete degree. Includes field trips, internships, and special projects. Job placement services available.

Admission
Admission selective. A total of 130 were enrolled in the B.F.A. program in fall 1990. Requires application, interview, and high school transcript.

Faculty
Shelle Barron, professor, communications graphics; Margaret Christensen, professor, communications graphics; Diane Crandall, professor, communications graphics; Francis Drake, professor, communications graphics; J. Roland Lafferty, professor, papermaking; Gopal Mitra, professor, printmaking; George Shoemaker, chairman, papermaking/book arts; Ian Short, professor, book arts, papermaking, printmaking; Susan Weimer, printmaking.

Expenses and Accommodations
$6,121 tuition, room, and board per year (state residents); $8,385 (nonresidents). $20 application fee. $600 art supplies and books (per year). Housing available.

Contact   Dr. George Shoemaker, Chairman
Art Department
Doucette Hall
Edinboro University
Edinboro, PA 16444
814-732-2406

Editorial Experts, Inc.
Alexandria, Virginia

WORKSHOPS IN WRITING, EDITING, PRODUCTION, AND MANAGEMENT

Sponsor
Training Division

Level
Professional

Program Objective
Designed to provide small-group, hands-on training for people in publications professions and others who may want training in writing, grammar, or desktop publishing.

Program Description
Workshops include Producing Newsletters with PageMaker, WordPerfect 5.1 Advanced Topics, Intensive Review of Grammar, Introduction to Proofreading and Copyediting, Building Speed and Accuracy in Proofreading, Editorial Proofreading, Strategies of Effective Writing, Revising and Editing Your Own Writing, User-Friendly Documentation, Writing and Editing for Science and Technology, Advanced Editing, Editorial Skills for Support Staff, Improving Editorial Skills, Intensive Introduction to Copyediting, Fundamentals of Indexing, Indexing Technical Materials, Preparing Winning Proposals, Production Techniques and Technology, The Printing Process, Quality Control in Publications, Estimating and Controlling Publications Costs, Managing the Publications Process, Creating Effective Newsletters, Introduction to Graphic Arts Materials and Techniques, Producing Newsletters with PageMaker, Ventura for Publications Professionals, and WordPerfect 5.1: The Basics. Half-day, full-day, or two-day classes meet weekdays. Each course grants continuing education unit (CEU) credit and certificate. Job placement services not available.

Admission
Admission open. Approximately 700 attended in 1990. Requires registration. Some classes require previous publishing experience.

Faculty
Faculty varies from year to year.

Expenses and Accommodations
$150–$550 per course. Housing not available.

Contact Sally Smith, Training Manager
Editorial Experts, Inc.
66 Canal Center Plaza
Alexandria, VA 22314
703-683-0683; fax 703-683-4915

Emerson College
Boston, Massachusetts

BACHELOR OF ARTS IN WRITING, LITERATURE, AND PUBLISHING

Sponsor
Department of Writing, Literature, and Publishing

Level
Undergraduate

Program Objective
Designed to meet the needs of students who are interested in pursuing careers as writers or as professionals in writing-related fields. Provides opportunities for interactive guided apprenticeships in professional writing and publishing.

Program Description
Courses include Literary Foundations, American Literature, British Literature, Advanced Professional Writing, Publication Practicum, Advertising Design, and Book Publishing. Completion of program leads to a B.A. in writing, literature, and publishing. Courses meet daytime. Undergraduate students typically take eight semesters to complete program. Includes internships and special projects. Job placement services available.

Admission
Admission selective. Application, essay, letters of reference, high school transcript recommended.

Faculty
James Randall, professor; Lynn Williams, professor; Jonathan Aaron, associate professor; Richard Duprey, associate professor; DeWitt Henry, chair; Robin Fast, associate professor; James Carroll, writer in residence; Dan Wakefield, writer in residence.

Expenses and Accommodations
$397 per credit (1991–92). $30 application fee. Housing available.

Contact   Office of Undergraduate and Graduate Admission
Emerson College
1 Arlington Street
Boston, MA 02114
617-578-8600 or 617-578-8610

Emerson College
Boston, Massachusetts

MASTER OF ARTS IN WRITING AND PUBLISHING

Sponsor
Department of Writing, Literature, and Publishing

Level
Graduate

Program Objective
Designed to meet the needs of students who are interested in pursuing careers as writers or as professionals in writing-related fields. Provides opportunities for interactive guided apprenticeships in professional writing and publishing.

Program Description
Courses include Literary Foundations, American Literature, British Literature, Advanced Professional Writing, Publication Practicum, Advertising Design, and Book Publishing. Completion of program leads to an M.A. in writing and publishing. Courses meet weekdays. Graduate students typically take four semesters to complete program. Includes internships and special projects. Job placement services available.

Admission
Admission selective. Application, essay, letters of reference, college transcript, undergraduate degree recommended.

Faculty
James Randall, professor; Lynn Williams, professor; Jonathan Aaron, associate professor; Richard Duprey, associate professor; DeWitt Henry, chair; Robin Fast, associate professor; James Carroll, writer in residence; Dan Wakefield, writer in residence.

Expenses and Accommodations
$397 per credit (1991–92). $30 application fee. Housing available.

Contact   Office of Undergraduate and Graduate Admission
Emerson College
1 Arlington Street
Boston, MA 02114
617-578-8600 or 617-578-8610

Front Range Community College
Westminster, Colorado

ELECTRONIC PUBLISHING PROGRAM

Sponsor
Department of Communications

Level
Undergraduate/Professional

Program Objective
The program prepares students for entry-level positions in electronic publishing.

Program Description
Courses include Desktop Publishing, Advanced Desktop Publishing, Graphic Arts for Writers, Technical Writing, and Introduction to Computers. Students select area of program emphasis: printing, office skills, or technical communication. Program leads to certificate. Requires completion of ten courses. Courses meet weekdays, evenings, weekends; students typically take three semesters to complete program. Requires computer literacy course be taken in the first semester. Includes field trips, internships, and special projects. Job placement services available.

Admission
Admission selective. In academic year 1990–91, 200 applied, 160 were accepted, 160 enrolled. Requires application, high school or college transcript.

Faculty
Bruce Frehner, instructor; Martha Plank, instructor; and Kathy Elliott, instructor.

Expenses and Accommodations
$1,290 for the entire program. $10 application fee. $50 other expenses. Housing available.

Contact   Office of Admissions
Front Range Community College
3645 West 112th Avenue
Westminster, CO 80030
303-466-8811; fax 303-466-1623

George Washington University
Washington, D.C.

PUBLICATION PROGRAMS

Sponsor
Center for Career Education and Workshops (CCEW)

Level
Professional

Program Objective
Designed to provide courses that cover the entire process of book, magazine, newsletter, and brochure publishing and desktop publishing.

Program Description
Publication specialist courses include Editing; Writing; Desktop Publishing; Graphic Design; Video Scriptwriting and Production; Newsletter, Magazine, and Book Publishing; and Publication Finance, Marketing and Management. Program awards Publication Specialist certificate, which requires completion of ten courses.

Desktop publishing specialist program trains individuals in the technical skills needed to use state-of-the-art electronic retrieval systems based on the traditional publishing concepts of design and production. Students learn on IBM and Macintosh systems. Upon successful completion of program, students are awarded Desktop Publishing Specialist certificate.

Courses meet evenings, weekdays, weekends; students typically take one to two years to complete program. Includes special projects. Job placement services available.

Admission
Admission open. Students must apply for certificate status. In 1990, 40 applied, 40 were accepted, 38 enrolled. Requires application, essay, interview, letters of reference, and high school or college transcript from certificate candidates. Undergraduate degree recommended.

Faculty
Richard Crum, senior writer, book division, National Geographic Society; Robert Thomas, visual information specialist (graphic design), President's Office at the White House; Les Greenberg, printing specialist, U.S. Government Printing Office; Sam Mok, comptroller, U.S. Department of the Treasury; Jim Sutton, marketing director, Naval Institute Press; Bita Lanys, president, Communicators Connection, Inc.; Elaine English, associate, Lichtman, Trister, Singer, and Ross.

Expenses and Accommodations
$321–$395 for individual courses. $2,700 plus fees for publication specialist program. $3,040 plus fees for desktop program. $25 application fee. $50 per course for textbooks. Housing not available.

Contact   Marilyn Millstone, Director
Publication Programs
George Washington University
2020 K Street, NW, B-100
Washington, DC 20052
202-994-5259; fax 202-296-2650

Graduate School and University Center of the City University of New York
New York, New York

EDUCATION IN PUBLISHING PROGRAM

Sponsor
Office of Special Programs

Level
Professional

Program Objective
A comprehensive, integrated program for adult learners that was developed from the basic curriculum by the Education for Publishing Committee of the Association of American Publishers.

Program Description
Courses include Copyediting and Proofreading; Line Editing; Production for the Nonspecialist; Book Promotion; International Publishing; Economics of Publishing; Marketing and Sales; Selling Subsidiary Rights; Children's Book Publishing; Book Publishing Law; Book Indexing; Research, Reference and Scholarly Publishing; Economics for the Small Press Publisher; Trade Book Publishing; and Direct Marketing of Books. Program awards certificate for satisfactory completion of each course. Courses meet evenings, spring and fall semesters, and are four to ten weeks long. Job placement services not available.

Admission
Admission open. In 1990–91, 120 applied, 120 were accepted, 120 enrolled. Requires application.

Faculty
All courses are taught by experienced publishing professionals. Instructors vary from semester to semester.

Expenses and Accommodations
$250–$275 per ten-week course (prorated for shorter courses). Application fee included in tuition. Housing not available.

Contact   Peg Rivers, Program Administrator
Education in Publishing Program
CUNY Graduate Center
Room 300
25 West 43rd Street
New York, NY 10036

Graphic Arts Association
Philadelphia, Pennsylvania

CONTINUING EDUCATION UNITS/CERTIFICATE PROGRAMS/MANAGEMENT CERTIFICATE PROGRAMS

Sponsor
Graphic Arts Education Center

Level
Professional

Program Objective
Designed for people entering the graphic arts industry or for those who are already working in the field but who lack career focus. Students may take structured continuing education courses in a variety of areas.

Program Description
Courses of study include graphic arts fundamentals, production, financial management, sales and management, IBM computer production and management, and Macintosh computer training. One continuing education unit (CEU) is earned for every ten hours of course participation; students who accumulate twelve CEUs or twenty-four CEUs receive Graphic Arts Institute Certificate of Achievement. Students who have successfully completed the required prerequisites may enroll in management certificate programs. Courses range from one to twelve weeks; center runs on a two-semester calendar. Field trips included. Job placement services available.

Courses are offered at the Graphic Arts Education Center and the University of the Arts, both in Philadelphia. Some courses are well suited to in-plant presentation, and arrangements may be made for on-site instruction.

Admission
Admission open. Application required. Certificate programs require college transcript.

Faculty
Faculty members are industry professionals.

Expenses and Accommodations
$135–$560 per course. Books range from $6–$55. Housing not available.

Contact   George Hess, Educational Director,
              or Jan Cassady, Evening School Registrar
         Graphic Arts Association
         1900 Cherry Street
         Philadelphia, PA 19103
         215-229-3313 or 215-229-3314

Graphic Arts Technical Foundation
Pittsburgh, Pennsylvania

INTRODUCTION TO COLOR AND PRINT PRODUCTION FOR DESKTOP PUBLISHERS

Sponsor
Technical Programs Department

Level
Professional

Program Objective
Designed to provide an overview of the printing processes and broad working knowledge of graphic communications, emphasizing color desktop and conventional production applications.

Program Description
Five-day workshop. Topics include the history of the printing process, camera operations, color reproduction basics, color separation, image assembly, the printing press, binding and finishing, design considerations and desktop layout methods, color on the desktop, high-end color, buying and specifying color, and cost estimating. Workshop meets weekdays. It is intended for graphic designers, corporate advertisers, and in-plant printing managers who want to know how the overall print production process and color reproduction are affected by desktop prepress techniques. Workshop awards certificate upon completion. Job placement services not available.

Admission
Admission open. Enrollment figures N/A.

Faculty
Faculty is composed of Graphic Arts Technical Foundation staff members who are experienced in desktop publishing and the commercial printing industry.

Expenses and Accommodations
$695–$905 per program. Housing not available.

Contact   James A. Workman, Director
Technical Programs
4615 Forbes Avenue
Pittsburgh, PA 15213
412-621-6941; fax 412-621-3049

Graphic Arts Technical Foundation
Pittsburgh, Pennsylvania

USING COLOR IN DESKTOP PUBLISHING, PRODUCTION, AND DESIGN

Sponsor
Technical Programs Department

Level
Professional

Program Objective
Designed to teach students about color theory and how to integrate software, hardware, and other components available from different vendors to assemble a custom-made system.

Program Description
Three-day workshop. Topics include conventional and electronic color proofing methods; mid-range and low-end color systems that scan, enhance, image, and proof; spot coloring black-and-white elements for ads and art; color separations; creating, separating, and processing elements with imagesetter technology; and conversion methods, data compressions, and file transfer techniques. Workshop meets weekdays. Intended for graphic designers, newspaper publishers, in-plant printers, and others interested in learning about the growing sophistication of desktop color. Workshop awards certificate upon completion. Job placement services not available.

Admission
Admission open. Enrollment figures N/A.

Faculty
Faculty is composed of Graphic Arts Technical Foundation staff members who are experienced in desktop publishing and the commercial printing industry.

Expenses and Accommodations
$695–$905 per program. Housing not available.

Contact   James A. Workman, Director
Technical Programs
4615 Forbes Avenue
Pittsburgh, PA 15213
412-621-6941; fax 412-621-3049

Guild of Book Workers
Washington, D.C.

STANDARD SEMINARS

Level
Professional

Program Objective
Designed to expose guild members and practitioners in the field of book arts to techniques in conservation, bookbinding, printing, and other book arts.

Program Description
Seminar topics vary from year to year and have included the logic behind German binding techniques, gold tooling and leather on-lay, and conservation rebacking. Each seminar consists of four workshops that meet on consecutive days. Job placement services not available.

Admission
Admission open to guild members on a space-available basis.

Faculty
Faculty varies from year to year.

Expenses and Accommodations
$90 per seminar (plus $40 membership fee). Other expenses include accommodations and meals.

Contact   Monique Lallier, Chairperson
Standard Seminars
12-A Park Village Lane
Greensboro, NC 27405
919-282-0624

Harvard University
Cambridge, Massachusetts

RADCLIFFE PUBLISHING COURSE

Sponsor
Radcliffe College

Level
Graduate/Professional

Program Objective
The total-immersion program is designed to provide entry into the field of publishing to graduating college seniors and people making career changes.

Program Description
Courses include Editing, The Literary Agent, Sales and Marketing, Publicity, Subsidiary Rights, Book Design and Production, Paperbacks, Academic Publishing, Textbooks, Book Packaging, Editorial Marketing, Children's Books, Magazine Ideas, Magazine Production and Design, Promotions, Circulation, Direct Mail, Advertising, Trade Magazines, Electronic Publishing, and Launching a New Magazine. Program awards certificate on completion of six-week course requirements. All students take the same full-time six-week summer program of lectures and workshops. Classes meet weekdays, evenings, and weekends. Students required to complete twelve written assignments prior to beginning the program. Includes field trips and special projects. Job placement services available.

Admission
Admission selective. In the academic year 1990–91, 300 applied, 95 were accepted, 91 enrolled. Requires application, essay, letters of reference, college transcript, undergraduate degree. Interview recommended.

Faculty
Faculty changes annually and is made up of well-known book and magazine publishing professionals.

Expenses and Accommodations
$2,965 per six-week program; $1,135 room and board. $35 application fee. Housing available.

Contact   Lindy Hess, Director
Radcliffe Publishing Course
Harvard University
77 Brattle Street
Cambridge, MA 02138
617-495-8678; fax 617-495-8422

Hofstra University
Hempstead, New York

PUBLISHING STUDIES AND LITERATURE CONCENTRATION

Sponsor
English Department

Level
Undergraduate

Program Objective
Designed to prepare English majors for careers in publishing by providing required studies in literature and instruction in copyediting, proofreading, line and manuscript editing.

Program Description
Courses include Theory and Practice of Publishing, History of Publishing in America, Book Editing I and II, Book Promotion, Editing Children's Books, Popular Literature and the Mass Market, Magazine Editing, Textbook Editing, Book Design and Production, Book Retailing, Books and the Law, and Economics of Publishing. Program leads to a B.A. in English. Requires completion of 39 credits in concentration. Classes meet evenings, weekdays, weekends; students generally complete major requirements in five semesters. Students must complete Composition I and II and pass the Writing Proficiency Test prior to beginning the program. Includes internships. Job placement services available.

Admission
Admission is open to all matriculated students. Enrollment figures N/A. Acceptance by the university requires application, letters of reference, high school transcript, and Scholastic Aptitude Test scores.

Faculty
Arthur Gregor, professor, English; Betty Bartleme, professor, English; Robert Carter, professor, English.

Expenses and Accommodations
$280 per credit. $25 application fee. Housing available.

Contact   Dr. Robert Sargent, Chairman
English Department
204 Calkins Hall
Hofstra University
Hempstead, NY 11550
516-463-5454

Houston Area Booksellers Association
Houston, Texas

HOUSTON AREA BOOKSELLERS ASSOCIATION SEMINARS

Level
Professional

Program Objective
Designed to increase the education, service, and profits of booksellers by instructing them in the fine points of bookselling—selling that extra copy and keeping the customer satisfied.

Program Description
Topics vary from seminar to seminar and have included hiring techniques, customer service, and loss prevention. Seminars are 1–1½ hours long; meet weekdays, evenings, weekends. Intended for bookstore managers and general staff. Job placement services not available.

Admission
Admission is open to members of the association. Enrollment ranges between 40 and 75.

Faculty
Speakers vary from seminar to seminar.

Expenses and Accommodations
$20 Houston Area Booksellers Associations annual membership fee. Housing not available.

Contact   Greg Newton, President
Houston Area Booksellers Association
c/o Sam Houston Bookshop
5015 Westheimer
Houston, TX 77056
713-626-1243

Howard University
Washington, D.C.

HOWARD UNIVERSITY PRESS BOOK PUBLISHING INSTITUTE

Sponsor
Howard University Press

Level
Graduate/Professional

Program Objective
To provide practical workshop and lecture sessions in every phase of book publishing for people interested in a career in publishing and for those in entry-level publishing jobs who want a broad overview of the field.

Program Description
Workshops include editing, design, marketing of scholarly books and trade books, and financial management. Lectures include the role of the editor, editor-author relations, the role of the literary agent, introduction to production, the role of the book manufacturer, subsidiary rights and permissions, introduction to marketing, the role of the bookseller, library and institutional markets, copyright and new technology, and desktop publishing. Includes sessions with publishing professionals to review student resumes and discuss career options. Program awards certificate of completion. Sessions meet weekdays, weekends during the summer; program takes five weeks to complete. Students required to complete reading and other assignments prior to beginning the program. Includes field trips and special projects. Job placement services available.

Admission
Admission selective. In the academic year 1990–91, 48 applied, 25 were accepted, 25 enrolled. Requires application, essay, letters of reference, college transcript, undergraduate degree, writing sample. Interview recommended.

Faculty
Faculty N/A.

Expenses and Accommodations
$1,850 tuition, room and board, books, and art supplies. $35 application fee. Housing available.

Contact Ms. Avis A. Taylor, Program Administrator
Howard University Press Book Publishing Institute
2900 Van Ness Street, NW
Washington, DC 20008
202-806-8465; fax 202-806-8474

The Huenefeld Company
Bedford, Massachusetts

1992 HUENEFELD BOOK PUBLISHING SEMINARS

Level
Professional

Program Objective
Designed to provide instruction on small-group dynamic systems to core managers (managers of acquisition, production, marketing, and business operations divisions) and publishers from publishing operations that have sales volumes of less than $20-million per year. Intended to upgrade the management skills of professionals already on the job and orient people aspiring to be managers or those new to their job to the skills that make the small-group dynamic successful.

Program Description
Editorial Planning, Acquisition, and Prepress Development of New Books is a two-day seminar for the editor-in-chief and the prepress managing editor. First day focuses on strategizing how many new titles and of what type they should seek over the next three years, how to find the authors to write them, and how to help those authors deliver on time. Second day explores the best ways to accomplish cost-effective copyediting, interior design, desktop camera-ready pages, printing specs, and bids. Job placement services not available.

Managing the Finances, Inventory, and Business Operations of Your Book Publishing House is a two-day seminar for the business manager and/or chief financial officer. Topics include administering the receivables and payables without rigid accounting software packages, how to track the cost and results of various segments of the publishing process, the ease and importance of annualizing data to eliminate seasonal distortions, credit and collections, profitability and adjustment, buying printing, managing the inventory investment, and optimal computer configurations for small organizations. Job placement services not available.

Planning and Performing Effective Book Marketing is a two-day seminar for the marketing manager. Topics include the basic marketing strategies that prove most effective for various types of publishers, coordinating the powerful one-two punch of promotion and selling, creating good promotional copy with less fuss and feathers, how publishers use telemarketing to combat the high cost of field sales representation, on-line order entry via the toll-free order phone, and business terms normal for different segments of the industry. Job placement services not available.

The Publisher's Job: Managing Book Publishing for Both Impact and Profits is a two-day seminar for publishers. Topics include how to recruit, nurture, and coordinate a core management team; simplified strategic planning to keep everybody moving in the same direction; what different types of publishers spend on acquisition, prepress, marketing, business operations, and management; how to calculate how many people are needed and what they should be paid; an easy database scheduling system that stimulates deadline discipline; and automatic performance indices to tell who's delivering the goods and who's not. Job placement services not available.

Special Concerns of Secular Not-for-Profit Publishers is a two-day seminar. Topics N/A. Job placement services not available.

Special Concerns of Religious Publishers (Commercial and Not-for-Profit) is a two-day seminar. Topics N/A. Job placement services not available.

Admission
Admission open on a space-available basis. Enrollment limited to 35 per seminar. Requires registration.

Faculty
John Huenefeld, editor/author, *The Huenefeld Report,* and senior publishing consultant, The Huenefeld Company.

Expenses and Accommodations
$450 per seminar. Other expenses include accommodations and meals.

Contact   The Huenefeld Company, Inc.
Box 665
Bedford, MA 01730
617-275-1070; fax 617-275-1713

Informative Edge
San Francisco, California

COLOR ON THE DESKTOP

Level
Professional

Program Objective
Designed to instruct Macintosh and PC users on how to obtain high-quality color output for printed materials.

Program Description
Courses in this training program include Publishing on Your PC, QuarkXpress for the Macintosh, Scanning Graphics and Text, Adobe Photoshop, and Aldus PageMaker. Program meets weekdays; training ranges from one to three days. Includes special projects. Job placement not available.

Admission
Admission open. Previous publishing experience recommended.

Faculty
Frank Catalano, director, Informative Edge.

Expenses and Accommodations
$695 per program. Housing not available.

Contact   Frank Catalano, Principal
100 Bush Street
Suite 845
San Francisco, CA 94104
415-392-5544; fax 415-392-3148

La Roche College
Pittsburgh, Pennsylvania

GRAPHIC ARTS PROGRAM

Sponsor
Graphic Design and Communication Department

Level
Undergraduate/Professional

Program Objective
Designed to train people to become managers in the graphic arts industry. Open to undergraduates who plan to enter the field and to professionals who want to improve their skills.

Program Description
Students pursuing a degree complete a three-component program. The graphics component includes courses in electronic publishing, graphic arts photography, typography, image assembly, paper and ink technology, offset press operation, estimating, and color separation. The management component includes courses in accounting, marketing, computers, finance, and personnel administration. The liberal arts component includes general liberal arts courses. Leads to a B.A. in graphic arts. Requires completion of 120 credits. Classes meet weekdays, evenings; students typically take four years to complete undergraduate degree. Nondegree students may take individual courses. Includes field trips, internships, and special projects. Job placement services available.

Admission
Admission to the college selective. Acceptance by the college requires application, high school transcript, and college transcript. Interview recommended.

Faculty
Tom Bates, associate professor, graphic arts.

Expenses and Accommodations
$7,138 tuition, $254 per credit. $25 application fee. Lab fees range from $50–$100; supplies range from $20–$100. Housing available.

Contact   Admissions Office
La Roche College
900 Babcock Boulevard
Pittsburgh, PA 15237
412-367-9241

La Roche College
Pittsburgh, Pennsylvania

GRAPHIC DESIGN PROGRAM

Sponsor
Graphic Design and Communication Department

Level
Undergraduate/Professional

Program Objective
Designed to train people who want to become designers of publications, electronic media, and advertising. Open to undergraduates who plan to enter the field and to professionals who want to improve their skills.

Program Description
Courses include basic design, art history, graphic design, typography, electronic art, and photography. Classes in management and liberal arts are required. Program leads to a B.A. in graphic design. Requires completion of 120 credits. Classes meet weekdays, evenings; students typically take four years to complete undergraduate degree. Nondegree students may take individual courses. Includes field trips, internships, and special projects. Job placement services available.

Admission
Admission to the college selective. Acceptance by the college requires application, high school transcript, and college transcript. Interview recommended.

Faculty
Martha Fairchild, professor, graphic design; Grant Dinsmore, professor, graphic design; George Founds, associate professor, graphic design; Tom Bates, associate professor, graphic arts.

Expenses and Accommodations
$7,138 tuition or $254 per credit. $25 application fee. Lab fees range from $50–$100; supplies range from $20–$100. Housing available.

Contact	Admissions Office
	La Roche College
	900 Babcock Boulevard
	Pittsburgh, PA 15237
	412-367-9241

La Salle University
Philadelphia, Pennsylvania

EDITING AND PUBLISHING

Sponsor
English Department

Level
Undergraduate

Course Objective
Hands-on course in editing and publishing. Designed to prepare students to do simple in-house publishing.

Course Description
This single course involves students in every part of in-house publishing—editing, writing, proofreading, and production. Students use Microsoft Word word processing and the Ventura Publisher to produce materials that range from flyers to brochures. Topics include functional writing, copyediting, proofreading, and desktop publishing. Course awards 3 credits. Course meets weekdays. Includes field trips and special projects. Job placement services available.

Admission
Admission selective; students must be enrolled at the university and have completed writing prerequisite. In academic year 1990–91, 28 applied, 24 were accepted, 24 enrolled. Enrollment at the university requires application, high school transcript, college transcript (if a transfer student). Interview recommended.

Faculty
John J. Keenan, professor, English.

Expenses and Accommodations
$10,250 tuition; $365 per credit hour. $20 application fee. $10 computer lab and incidentals fee. Housing available.

Contact   John J. Keenan, Professor of English
LaSalle University
1900 West Olney Avenue
Philadelphia, PA 19141
215-951-1151; fax 215-951-1892

Magazine Publishers of America
New York, New York

MPA PROFESSIONAL DEVELOPMENT SEMINARS

Sponsor
MPA Education Department

Level
Professional

Program Objective
Designed to prepare people as they begin careers in magazine publishing and to provide established professionals with continuing professional development. Seminars, workshops, and conferences are dedicated to disseminating new ideas across the entire spectrum of the magazine publishing enterprise.

Program Description
Year-round program includes workshops, roundtables, day-long seminars, and multi-day conferences. Topics cover the full range of areas involved in magazine publishing—management, editorial, advertising sales and marketing, production, design, desktop publishing, and circulation and fulfillment. Some are targeted for entry-level staffers and some for experienced personnel and executive management. Classes meet weekdays. Some seminars require assignments to be completed in advance. Internships are available as a separate MPA Education Department activity. Job placement services not available.

Recent seminar topics included Integrated Sales, What Is an Employee?, How to Read Your Buyer and Sell More Pages, Fundamentals of Magazine Circulation, Making Presentations That Sell, Magazine Accounting . . . A Primer, Problem Solving and Closings, Effective Marketing and Promotion for Smaller Publishers, Listening, Circulation Marketing Conference, Financial Conference, Sales Letters That Sell, Media Research, Circulation Accounting, Legal Update, Motivating Your Sales Staff in Tough Times, The Copy Masters, Magazine Publishing Congress, Magazine Publishing Procedures, and The Basics of Editorial Research.

Admission
Admission open. Previous publishing experience recommended.

Faculty
Most presenters are consultants to the magazine industry or industry professionals.

Expenses and Accommodations
$100–$145 for half-day seminars. Housing not available.

Contact   Diane Cremin, Education Associate
Magazine Publishers of America
575 Lexington Avenue
Suite 540
New York, NY 10022
212-752-0055; fax 212-888-4217

Midsouth Booksellers Association
Bartlesville, Oklahoma

MIDSOUTH BOOKSELLERS ASSOCIATION SEMINARS

Level
Professional

Program Objective
Designed to help booksellers better handle the day-to-day problems of their business and to educate them and librarians about specific issues in the field.

Program Description
Recent seminar topics included managing bookstores, training employees, financial statements, balance sheets, selecting children's books for fall and the Christmas season, selecting books for long-range education programs, buying books from wholesalers, and customer service. The seminars, three days long, meet Friday/Saturday/Sunday. Job placement services not available.

Admission
Admission open. Total enrollment for the 1990 seminars was 200.

Faculty
Instructors are members of the New York–based American Booksellers Association.

Expenses and Accommodations
$25 per seminar. Attendees are required to arrange their own accommodations and meals.

Contact   Betty J. Duding, President
Midsouth Booksellers Association
554 S.E. Washington
Bartlesville, OK 74006
918-333-7262

Milwaukee Area Technical College
Milwaukee, Wisconsin

PRINTING AND PUBLISHING—OPERATIONS

Sponsor
Business and Graphic Arts Division

Level
Undergraduate

Program Objective
This two-year associate degree program is designed to prepare individuals for employment in the graphic arts/printing industry.

Program Description
Courses include Applied Science for Graphic Communications, Graphic Production Processes, Finishing Operations, Press Production Problems 1 and 2, Typography Workshop 1 and 2, Halftone Techniques, Lithography, Materials of Printing Production, Introduction to Printing Estimating, Basic Color Scanner Operation, Customer Service Representative/Print Marketing and Sales, Design 1, Fundamental Photography, Graphic Communication Processes, Production Planning and Control, Copy Preparation and Markup, Introduction to Desktop Publishing, Advanced Color Scanner Operation, Printing Estimating Workshop, Special Projects in Printing, and An Active Approach to Wellness and Fitness. Program leads to associate degree in applied science. Requires twenty-four courses (64 semester credits, including 15 general education credits). Courses meet weekdays, evenings; students typically take four semesters to complete program. Includes field trips, internships, and special projects. Job placement services available.

Admission
Admission selective. In academic year 1990–91, 183 applied, 110 were accepted, 73 enrolled. Admission to the college requires application, high school transcript, admission testing. Recommends interview and, for transfer students, college transcript.

Faculty
Dewey Coerper, Sharman Hummel, Ted Joyce, Gerhard Lang, Leonard McGhee, James McKenzie, Walter Royek, Neal Schuster, Ryan Smith, Anne Steinberg.

Expenses and Accommodations
$41 per credit hour. Housing not available.

Contact   Michael Walsh, Associate Dean
Milwaukee Area Technical College
700 West State Street
Milwaukee, WI 53233
414-278-6252; fax 414-271-2195

National Association of College Stores
Oberlin, Ohio

GENERAL BOOKS SEMINAR

Sponsor
NACS Education Committee

Level
Professional

Program Objective
Designed to enhance general bookselling and to teach general book buyers how to improve their performance.

Program Description
Topics include how general books are published, planning a general book department, budgeting and inventory management, buying, merchandising, promotional books, customer service, receiving, pricing, and stock control. Program awards certificate of completion. Seminar lasts from three to five days; meets weekdays, evenings, weekends. Job placement services not available.

Admission
Admission open.

Faculty
Faculty is composed of college-store industry professionals.

Expenses and Accommodations
$450 per seminar. Housing available.

Contact   Barbara Bushman, Assistant Director
Education
National Association of College Stores
500 E. Lorain Street
Oberlin, OH 44074-1298
216-775-7777; fax 216-775-4769

National Association of Independent Publishers
Moore Haven, Florida

PUBLISHING SEMINARS

Level
Professional

Program Description
Seminars for small and independent presses are designed to instruct start-up publishers and established publishers on promotion, marketing, and sales. Held on weekends, typically from noon on Friday to noon on Sunday.

Admission
Admission open.

Faculty
Seminars are taught by experienced publishing professionals. Recent speakers included Sarah Goodman, publishing and entertainment attorney; Dr. Jeffery Lant, publishing and marketing consultant, JLA Publications; Joe Sabah, publishing and marketing consultant; and Michael Isom, president, Unique Books.

Expenses and Accommodations
$50–$200 per seminar. Other expenses include accommodations and meals.

Contact   Betty Wright, Director
National Association of Independent Publishers
P.O. Box 850
Moore Haven, FL 33471
813-946-0293; fax 813-944-0293

National Association of Printers and Lithographers
Teaneck, New Jersey

MANAGEMENT INSTITUTE

Sponsor
Center for Continuing Education

Level
Graduate/Professional

Program Objective
Designed to help printing executives effectively handle the specific problems and decisions they face on the job by using a combination of theoretical and practical management techniques.

Program Description
Three disciplines are covered in individual six-day sessions held simultaneously each year the first week of June: marketing, business planning, and production management. Instruction includes case studies, projects, and group discussions. Successful completion of one course results in certification in that area. Successful completion of all three courses results in Certified Graphic Arts Executive award. Classes meet weekdays, evenings. Students must complete reading assignments prior to beginning the program. Includes special projects. Job placement services not available.

Topics in marketing include identifying marketing needs and developing strategies to meet them, gathering marketing intelligence, developing pricing strategies, coordinating between customer services and marketing advances, and estimating the cost and measuring the effectiveness of a marketing plan.

Topics in business planning include planning for future growth; gaining management and staff support; balancing the needs of marketing, finance, and production; planning for technological change; assigning accountability; and assessing company performance.

Topics in production management include addressing customer concerns, achieving maximum productivity, increasing efficiency, motivating personnel, controlling inventory, buying equipment, managing on-the-job stress, developing effective cost controls, and understanding new technology.

Admission
Admission open to those with previous publishing experience. Application required.

Faculty
Faculties are composed of instructors from university business management schools and graphic arts schools in the United States and Canada and of professionals from industry.

Expenses and Accommodations
$3,100 per course (NAPL members); $3,400 (nonmembers). Includes housing.

Contact   Lee-Ann M. Fischer, Special Projects Manager
National Association of Printers and Lithographers
780 Palisade Avenue
Teaneck, NJ 07666
201-342-0706; fax 201-692-1862

New England Booksellers Association
Boston, Massachusetts

NEBA BOOKSELLING SEMINARS

Level
Professional

Program Objective
Designed to help booksellers and prospective booksellers increase their sales.

Program Description
The seminar program changes yearly. Recent topics included personnel management issues, the financial aspects of a bookstore, ordering merchandise, selling computer books, and increasing outside sales. Seminars held weekends, partial day. Job placement services not available.

Admission
Admission open. NEBA membership recommended.

Faculty
Speakers are bookstore owners and managers and trade book authors.

Expenses and Accommodations
Seminar fees range from nothing to $80.

Contact   New England Booksellers Association
45 Newbury Street
Suite 506
Boston, MA 02116
1-800-466-8711; fax 617-421-9341

New York City Technical College of the City University of New York, Center for Advertising, Printing, and Publishing
Brooklyn, New York

GRAPHIC ARTS PRODUCTION MANAGEMENT

Sponsor
Graphic Arts and Advertising Technology

Level
Undergraduate

Program Objective
Designed to meet the growing needs of people working in or entering publishing, printing, or advertising industries by teaching skills via applied laboratory projects and using industry standards.

Program Description
Over forty courses in related graphic arts production are available to satisfy one-, two-, and four-year degree requirements. Program can lead to certificate in computer-aided advertising and publishing (two semesters full-time), associate degree in production or technology (four semesters full-time), and bachelor's degree in graphic arts production management (eight semesters full-time). Courses meet weekdays, evenings. Requires outside reading and laboratory projects. Includes field trips, internships, and special projects. Job placement services available.

Admission
Admission is open. Requires application and high school or college transcript.

Faculty
12 full-time faculty members, 5 technicians, and 8–15 adjunct professors.

Expenses and Accommodations
$2,000 tuition per year; $57 per credit. $30 application fee. $1,000 for books and supplies. Housing not available.

Contact   Dr. James P. DeLuca, Chairman
Center for Advertising, Printing, and
   Publishing
New York City Technical College of the City
   University of New York
300 Jay Street
Brooklyn, NY 11201-2983
718-260-5822; fax 718-260-5198

New York Institute of Technology
Old Westbury, New York

BOOK DESIGN

Sponsor
Fine Art Department

Level
Undergraduate

Course Objective
Designed to provide an introduction to creative book construction including layout and illustration, for senior-level students. Students examine traditional bookbinding methods and new book forms as they relate to contemporary graphic design and publishing needs.

Course Description
Course requires students to construct a hand-sewn book; design an original binding with block or screened endpapers; experiment with designing, forming, and collating the art content of a spiral binder; and design and write a stapled instruction manual. Four-credit senior-level course meets once a week for four weeks. Requires students to complete prerequisite courses in typography and design fundamentals. Includes field trips and special projects. Job placement services not available.

Admission
Admission is open to matriculated students. Admission to the institute is selective and requires application, interview, high school transcript, college transcript (if transfer student), and portfolio review. Enrollment figures N/A.

Faculty
Felix Zbarsky, adjunct professor, fine arts; Shirley Marein, professor, fine arts.

Expenses and Accommodations
$225 per credit. $20 application fee. $30 supplies. Housing available.

Contact   Shirley Marein, Professor
Fine Art Department
New York Institute of Technology
Old Westbury, NY 11568
516-686-7542

New York University
New York, New York

BOOK PUBLISHING CERTIFICATE PROGRAM

Sponsor
Center for Publishing

Level
Professional

Program Objective
Designed to offer noncredit courses for beginning and advanced publishing professionals and for people interested in changing careers. Courses range from teaching specific skills to in-depth examinations of particular publishing areas.

Program Description
Courses include Book Publishing Overview, Editing, Copyediting and Proofreading, Children's Publishing, The Literary Agent, Book Design, Line Editing, Book Financials, History of Book Publishing, Publicity, Indexing, Subsidiary Rights, Publishing Law, Book Production, Marketing, Book Packaging, Illustrated Books, Guide to Bookselling, Audio, and Starting a Career in Book Publishing. Program awards certificate. Requires completion of six courses. Courses meet evenings; students take three to six semesters to complete program. Includes field trips. Faculty may provide job leads; job openings posted.

Admission
Admission open. Undergraduate degree recommended.

Faculty
Marc Aronson, editor, HarperCollins; Lisa Berkowitz, book publicity consultant; Joe Blades, executive editor, Ballantine Books; Ann Cahn, special projects copyeditor, Morrow; Marsha Cohen, designer/illustrator, Parallelogram Graphic Communications; Sydney Cohen, president, S. W. Cohen & Associates, Inc.; Bartholomew D'Andrea, president, Meadow Graphic Systems; George Davidson, vice president and director/production operations, Ballantine/Del Rey/Fawcett Books; Maria Epes, art director, Chelsea House Publishers; Mary Evans, agent, Virginia Barber Literary Agency; Ellen Faran, CFO and general manager, Farrar, Straus & Giroux; Greg Giangrande, personnel representative, Random House; Peter L. Ginsberg, president, Curtis Brown, Ltd.; Lisa Healy, executive editor, Donald I. Fine, Inc.; Andrew Hoffer, production and art director, Donald I. Fine, Inc.; Miriam Hurewitz, free-lance copyeditor, proofreader, and editorial consultant; Beena Kamlani, senior production editor/trade, Viking Penguin; Heather Kliemann, director/subsidiary rights, Walt Disney Publishers; Tisa Lynn Lerner, creative director/partner, PLK Graphics, Inc.; Sandra MacGowan, vice president/editorial services, First Boston Corp.; Joan Marlow, free-lance copyeditor; Anthony Meisel, managing director, AM Publishing Services; Belle Newton, book publicity consultant; Patty O'Connell, free-lance line editor; Pamela Pollock, senior editor, Simon & Schuster Books for Young Readers; Katherine Rowe, attorney, Lankenau & Bickford; Linda Stern, free-lance editor; Sona Vogel, free-lance editorial consultant, line editor and copyeditor, and proofreader; and Jane von Mehren, senior editor, Ticknor & Fields.

Expenses and Accommodations
$1,500 per program ($225–$300 per course). Housing not available.

Contact   Janatha Pollock, Assistant Director
Center for Publishing
New York University
48 Cooper Square
New York, NY 10003
212-998-7220; fax 212-995-5771

New York University
New York, New York

MAGAZINE PUBLISHING DIPLOMA PROGRAM

Sponsor
Center for Publishing

Level
Graduate/Professional

Program Objective
Designed to provide integrated training in all facets of magazine publishing. The focus is on management with a practical skills orientation. The program is appropriate for junior-level publishing personnel and middle managers who are looking for broader understanding of the publishing process.

Program Description
Courses include Magazine Publishing Management; Advertising, Sales, Research, and Promotion; Editing; Production and Manufacturing; Circulation; Magazine Design and Art Direction; Strategic Computer Modeling; and Master Class in Magazine Editing. Program awards a diploma. Requires completion of six courses. Courses meet evenings; students typically take three to six semesters to complete program. Includes field trips and special projects. Faculty members serve as career counselors and may provide job leads.

Admission
Admission selective. In academic year 1990–91, 66 applied, 60 were accepted, 44 enrolled. Requires application, essay, letters of reference, college transcript. One year of publishing experience recommended.

Faculty
David Abrahamson, president, Enfield Research/Editorial Consultants; Thomas Edwards, director/client services and marketing, Ladd Associates; Peter Kines, marketing director, *Architectural Digest;* Shirrel Rhoades, publisher, *Opportunity, Income Plus;* Richard Sasso, vice president/production and distribution, *Scientific American;* Kitty Williams, vice president/circulation, *Business Week;* Fo Wilson, creative director, Studio W.

Expenses and Accommodations
$6,800 for entire program. $15 application fee. Other expenses include approximately $500 for books and materials. Housing not available.

Contact   Janatha Pollock, Assistant Director
Center for Publishing
New York University
48 Cooper Square
New York, NY 10003
212-998-7220; fax 212-995-5771

New York University
New York, New York

SUMMER INSTITUTE IN BOOK AND MAGAZINE PUBLISHING

Sponsor
Center for Publishing

Level
Graduate/Professional

Program Objective
Designed for college seniors and recent graduates who want to master the skills needed to enter the book and magazine publishing industries.

Program Description
The six-week full-time course includes lectures and workshops in manuscript evaluation, copyediting and proofreading, promotion, publicity, design, marketing, budgeting, and negotiating. Covers trade book, paperback, textbook, university press, reference, and children's book publishing. Features editors, publishers, agents, marketers, designers, and art directors as guest speakers and workshop leaders. Program awards certificate. Classes meet weekdays for six weeks. Includes field trips. Job fair, job postings, and resume and interviewing workshops.

Admission
Admission selective. In calendar year 1990, 102 applied, 70 were accepted, 59 enrolled. Requires application, essay, letters of reference, college transcript.

Faculty
Carol Meyer, Book Institute coordinator; Patrice Adcroft, Magazine Institute coordinator.

Expenses and Accommodations
$3,000 for entire program. $35 application fee. Housing available.

Contact   Janatha Pollock, Assistant Director
Center for Publishing
New York University
48 Cooper Square
New York, NY 10003
212-998-7220; fax 212-995-5771

Northwestern University, Medill School of Journalism
Evanston, Illinois

MAGAZINE PUBLISHING PROJECT

Sponsor
Graduate Editorial Division

Level
Graduate/Professional

Program Objective
Designed to mirror the launching of a new periodical, the eleven-week course examines every aspect of magazine publishing from conceiving a magazine to publishing a 48-page prototype of it, including forming a staff.

Program Description
Aided by 6 or 7 instructors, a group of no more than 20 students forms a working staff and creates a viable magazine concept, developing editorial and design elements, reader survey, media kit, sales campaign, circulation and business plans, and a financial prospectus. The seminar includes training in advanced reporting and writing, issue pacing, editorial calendar, and article mix. After the prototype's assumptions are presented to magazine executives and the magazine is published, 2,000 copies are distributed to alumni, academics, and media professionals. Program is the final quarter of a three-quarter M.S. in journalism program. Classes meet weekdays, evenings, weekends; project lasts eleven weeks. Students required to complete the other two quarters of M.S. requirements, including public affairs reporting, government and the news media, and magazine writing and editing workshop. Includes field trips. Job placement services available.

Admission
Admission selective. In calendar year 1991, 78 applied, 41 were accepted, 37 enrolled in the M.S. program. Requires application, essay, letters of reference, college transcript, undergraduate degree, Graduate Record Examinations scores. Interview recommended.

Faculty
Abe Peck, associate professor and chair, Magazine Program; Bernard Gordon, visiting associate professor of journalism and president of Bernard Gordon & Associates.

Expenses and Accommodations
$3,779 per quarter. $50 application fee. Other expenses include $2,915 per quarter for room and board, books, transportation, personal expenses, and health insurance. Housing available.

Contact   Abe Peck, Chair
Magazine Program
Medill School of Journalism
1845 Sheridan Road
Northwestern University
Evanston, IL 60208-2101
708-491-2068; fax 708-491-5907

Pace University
New York, New York

MASTER OF SCIENCE IN PUBLISHING PROGRAM

Sponsor
English Department

Level
Graduate

Program Objective
Designed to educate students in all aspects of the publishing business: finance, production, sales and marketing, the legal intricacies of acquisitions and subsidiary rights, editing, and production.

Program Description
Courses include Principles of Publishing, Book Production, Magazine Production, Financial Aspects of Publishing, Subsidiary Rights, Information Systems in Publishing, Editorial Principles and Practices, and Graduate Seminar or Internship. Electives include Specialized Publications, Distribution Methods, Legal Aspects of Publishing, Modern Technology in Publishing, Seminar on Books and Magazines, Magazine Circulation, Magazine Advertising Sales, Magazine Writing and Editing, Professional Editing, and Publishing Business Communication Skills. Program awards M.S. in publishing. Requires completion of 36 credits. Classes meet weekdays; full-time students typically take three semesters to complete program, and part-time students take five. Includes internships, special projects. Job placement services available.

Admission
Admission selective. In 1990–91, 60 applied, 40 were accepted, 28 enrolled. Requires application, essay, letters of reference, college transcript, undergraduate degree.

Faculty
Stevan Baron, vice president/production, *Aperture,* and director/art and production, Industrial Press; Ilene Berson Weiner, magazine production consultant; Edgar Buttenheim, former executive vice president, Springhouse Corporation, and advisory board member, M.S. in publishing program; Robert Carter, consultant, author, and director of internships, M.S. in publishing program; Peter Hanson, former publisher, *Money* and *Home Mechanix;* Berenice Hoffman, literary agent; Mark Hussey, author, assistant professor, Department of English, and chair, editorial committee of the Pace University Press; Karla Jay, professor, Department of English; Harry Johnson, vice president and general counsel, Magazine Group, Time, Inc.; Berton Leiser, distinguished professor of philosophy; Karen Mayer, general counsel, Putnam Berkley Group, Inc.; Margaret Nichols, managing editor, *Field & Stream;* Allan Rabinowitz, professor of accounting and associate director and advisory board member, M.S. in publishing program; Eliot Schein, president, Schein/Blattstein Advertising, Inc.; Ivor Whitson, president, CenterLink Information Systems, and advisory board member, M.S. in publishing program; Veronica Whitson, adjunct lecturer, Department of English.

Expenses and Accommodations
$355 per credit. $45 application fee. Housing available.

Contact   Sherman Raskin, Chairman
Department of English
Pace University
Pace Plaza
New York, NY 10038
212-346-1417; fax 212-346-1719

Pacific Lutheran University
Tacoma, Washington

PUBLISHING AND PRINTING ARTS PROGRAM

Sponsor
English Department

Level
Undergraduate

Program Objective
The program is intended to equip people considering careers in publishing with the critical perspectives and practical skills needed in the field and to examine, in a liberal arts context, the aesthetic, historical, sociological, and commercial dimensions of contemporary publishing and book culture.

Program Description
Required courses are The Book in Society, The Art of the Book I, and Publishing Procedures. Electives are chosen from at least two of the following three categories: editing/writing, design/ production, and marketing/management. The program is an interdisciplinary minor meant to supplement any bachelor's degree program. Requires completion of six courses. Classes meet weekdays, evenings; students typically take two to four semesters to complete program. Includes field trips, internships, and special projects. Job placement services available.

Admission
Admission open to all students at the university; nonmatriculated students may enroll in individual courses. Interview and acceptance to the university are recommended. Instructor's permission needed to enroll in individual courses.

Faculty
All courses are taught by the faculty in the departments of art, communication arts, business, and English.

Expenses and Accommodations
$1,200 per course. Housing available to full-time students.

Contact   Megan Benton, Director
Publishing and Printing Arts Program
Department of English
Pacific Lutheran University
Tacoma, WA 98447
206-535-8774; fax 206-535-8320

Parsons School of Design
New York, New York

CERTIFICATE AND DEGREE PROGRAMS

Sponsor
Continuing Education

Level
Undergraduate/Professional

Program Objective
The courses are intended to provide students with technical and design expertise.

Program Description
Courses include book design, book jacket design, magazine design, catalog and brochure design, promotion design, and production. Programs lead to an associate degree or a certificate. Degree programs require completion of 65 credits; certificate requires completion of ten courses. Classes meet weekdays, evenings, weekends. Includes field trips and special projects. Job placement services available.

Admission
Admission open. Requires application, interview, high school transcript, college transcript.

Expenses and Accommodations
$408 per credit; $298 per noncredit course. Housing available.

Contact   Donal Higgins, Associate Dean
Parsons School of Design
66 Fifth Avenue
New York, NY 10011
212-229-8933; fax 212-229-2456

Printing Industries of America, Inc.
Alexandria, Virginia

PIA EXECUTIVE DEVELOPMENT PROGRAM

Sponsor
Member Programs

Level
Professional

Program Objective
Designed to provide industry-specific training to graphic arts professionals.

Program Description
Management training program comprised of two 9-day sessions: First Year and Senior Year. Sessions run concurrently. Certificates are awarded upon successful completion of each. Successful completion of the full program results in 13.9 continuing education units (CEUs). Includes special projects. Job placement services not available.

First Year topics include finance, accounting, organizational management, quality improvement, sales and marketing. Students experience the role of the printing manager through the use of a hands-on printing management computer simulation program.

Senior Year topics include strategies for decision making, marketing planning and positioning, legal environment, management and leadership styles, performance evaluation and appraisals, communications, and financial and economic analysis. Students also develop, present, and defend a complete business plan.

Graduate Executive Development Program for certified EDP graduates is also available. Topic of the three-day program changes yearly.

Admission
Admission open. No prerequisites for First Year program. Senior Year students must have completed first-year course. Graduate program students must be certified graduates of the first and senior year courses. In 1990, 155 applied, 155 were accepted, 133 enrolled. Requires registration. Previous publishing experience recommended.

Faculty
Faculty is composed of printing industry executives and consultants.

Expenses and Accommodations
$2,250 per nine-day session (PIA member); $3,000 (nonmember). $975 graduate program (PIA member); $1,275 (nonmember). Includes housing, meals, and airport transfers.

Contact   Diane E. Swanson, Manager
Educational Services
Printing Industries of America, Inc.
100 Daingerfield Road
Alexandria, VA 22314-2888
703-519-8125; fax 703-548-3227

Rice University
Houston, Texas

RICE UNIVERSITY PUBLISHING PROGRAM

Sponsor
Continuing Studies

Level
Undergraduate/Graduate/Professional

Program Objective
To develop the talent and skills of people interested in a career in book or magazine publishing.

Program Description
The four-week program is divided into two sections: book publishing and magazine publishing. In book publishing, students assume the principal roles in simulated publishing houses, read actual manuscripts, choose titles for publication lists, and produce a prospectus (including budget and advertising plans). In magazine publishing, students also work in groups to develop a magazine concept, learn about budgets, circulation, advertising, and promotion, and present a mock-up of a prototype. Awards certificate of completion. Classes meet weekdays, evenings. Prior to beginning the program, students are given reading and research assignments. Job placement services not available.

Admission
Admission selective. In academic year 1990–91, 110 applied, 90 were accepted, 61 enrolled. Requires application, essay, letters of reference, college transcript. College degree recommended.

Faculty
Jack McKeown, publisher, Simon & Schuster; Carol Schneider, vice president and director/publicity, Random House; Kris Kliemann, director/subsidiary rights, Disney Publishing; Seth Hoyt, publisher, *Cosmopolitan;* Fred Woodward, art director, *Rolling Stone;* Jonathan Van Meter, senior editor, *Vogue.*

Expenses and Accommodations
$1,575 per four-week program. $20 application fee. Housing available.

Contact   Edie Carlson-Abbey, Assistant Dean/Director of Programs
Continuing Studies
Rice University
P.O. Box 1892
Houston, TX 77251-1892
713-527-4803; fax 713-285-5213

Rochester Institute of Technology
Rochester, New York

M.S. IN PUBLISHING

Sponsor
School of Printing Management and Sciences

Level
Graduate

Program Objective
The program is designed to prepare students to enter the printing industry at the management level and emphasizes technical prepress management.

Program Description
Courses cover all aspects of printing technology, electronic prepress management, electronic desktop to prepress systems, magazine publication, and typography and aesthetics. Program leads to M.S. degree. Classes meet weekdays, evenings; students typically take four quarters to complete program. Prior to the beginning of the program, students must complete foundation courses, which include typography, design, accounting systems, composition technology, printing processes, basic computer, planning and finishing, math science, and graphic imaging technique. Individual courses may be waived if student has prior experience in the subject. Foundation courses held in summer. Job placement services available.

Admission
Admission selective. In academic year 1991–92, 26 applied, 21 were accepted, 17 enrolled. Requires application, letters of reference, college transcript, undergraduate degree. Interview, previous publishing experience recommended.

Faculty
N/A

Expenses and Accommodations
$12,657 per year; $359 per credit hour. $35 application fee. Other expenses include approximately $8,000 for room and board, books, and lab materials. Housing available.

Contact   Marie Freckleton, Coordinator
Publishing Graduate Program
School of Printing Management and Sciences
Rochester Institute of Technology
1 Lomb Memorial Drive
Rochester, NY 14623
716-475-5871

Rocky Mountain Book Publishers Association
Boulder, Colorado

BOOK LORE SEMINARS

Level
Professional

Program Objective
Designed to help in the professional development of small full-time publishers. Planned as an extension of the RMBPA Annual Conference, the Book Lore seminars cover the four basic areas of publishing: editing, administration, production, and marketing.

Program Description
Topics of the seminars and colloquiums change yearly. Recent seminars included Marketing Problems for Small Publishers and The First Amendment and the Publisher. Colloquiums address industry issues. Meet evenings.

Admission
Admission open to RMBPA members and friends. In 1990, approximately 25 attended each seminar. RMBPA membership requires individuals to have put three books into print—one of those in the last two years.

Faculty
Speakers vary according to topic.

Expenses and Accommodations
$5 per seminar. $75 annual RMBPA membership fee.

Contact   Alan Stark, Executive Director
Rocky Mountain Book Publishers Association
755 Brook Road
Boulder, CO 80302
303-652-3926

School of Visual Arts
New York, New York

GRAPHIC DESIGN

Sponsor
Graphic Design

Level
Undergraduate/Professional

Program Objective
To develop an artist who can create art that effectively meets the ideas and needs of other people and who understands that to create art of any kind a personal creative process is required.

Program Description
Courses include Publishing Design, Experimental Book Art, Headlines and Visuals, Editorial Design, and Designing with Typography. Leads to bachelor's degree. Nonmatriculated students who have a bachelor's degree in art may take courses for no credit. Classes meet weekdays, evenings; students typically take eight 12-week semesters to complete program. Includes internships and special projects. Job placement services available.

Admission
Admission selective. In 1990–91, 868 applied, 588 were accepted, 492 enrolled. Admission to the school requires application, essay, interview, high school transcript, college transcript, portfolio.

Faculty
Richard Wilde, chair, graphic design/advertising; Christopher Austopchuk, art director, CBS Records; Paul Bacon, specialist in book jacket design; E. E. Benguiat, creative director, Photolettering, Inc.; George Fernandez, illustrator, Ballantine/Fawcett and Doubleday; Milton Glaser, president, Milton Glaser, Inc., cofounder of *New York Magazine*.

Expenses and Accommodations
$10,500 tuition per year. $25 application fee. Other expenses include room, board, books, and class materials. Housing available.

Contact   Martha Schindler, Director of Admissions
School of Visual Arts
209 East 23rd Street
New York, NY 10010-3994
212-679-7350; fax 212-725-3587

Simmons College
Graduate School of Library and
Information Science
Boston, Massachusetts

MODERN PUBLISHING AND LIBRARIANSHIP

Sponsor
Graduate School of Library and Information Science

Level
Graduate/Professional

Course Objective
Designed to examine the publishing industry and its relation to the library profession.

Course Description
Single 4-credit course covers history and modern process of publication, including editing, design, selection, typography, composition, printing, illustration, binding, marketing, methods of distribution, and sales outlets. Also covers organization and current issues in the publishing industry, problems in acquisitions, copyright, and specialized publishing. Includes field trips. Job placement services available.

Admission
Admission to the Graduate School is selective. Candidates must apply for the master's degree program, which requires application, undergraduate degree, college transcript, letters of reference, essay. Requirements for unclassified students include M.L.S. from an American Library Association–accredited school, transcript, application. Unclassified students may take up to 8 credits. Course may be taken as an elective. The course is also open to alumni for credit or audit, to students in other ALA-accredited graduate programs for credit, and to graduates of other ALA-accredited master's degree programs for credit.

Faculty
Anita Silvey, editor-in-chief, Horn Book.

Expenses and Accommodations
$426 per credit. Simmons M.L.S. graduates may audit for half tuition.

Contact   Judith Beals, Director of Admissions
Graduate School of Library and Information Science
Simmons College
300 The Fenway
Boston, MA 02115-5898
617-738-2264

Southern Illinois University
Carbondale, Illinois

BOOK PUBLISHING INTERNSHIP

Sponsor
Southern Illinois University Press

Level
Undergraduate/Graduate

Program Objective
Designed to train people who have no previous experience in the field for a career in book publishing. Interns are given an overview of the industry and hands-on experience in each facet of publishing.

Program Description
In the two-semester Press Internship, interns learn the basics of publishing—manuscript editing, book design, and marketing—through working on actual books in progress at SIU Press. Nine credit hours toward bachelor's or master's degree. Students should read *Edit Yourself* prior to the fall term. Includes field trips and special projects. Job placement services not available.

Admission
Admission selective. In academic year 1991–92, 15 applied, 4 were accepted, 4 enrolled. Interns need not be full-time matriculated students. Requires application, essay, interview, college transcript.

Faculty
Dr. Carol A. Burns, project editor, Southern Illinois University Press; James D. Simmons, associate director/marketing, Southern Illinois University Press; Natalia Nadraga, assistant director/production, Southern Illinois University Press.

Expenses and Accommodations
$677 for 6 credit hours (fall term); $420 for 3 credit hours (spring term). Rates for nonresidents slightly higher. Other expenses include approximately $50 for *Chicago Manual of Style* and *MLA Guide*. Housing available.

Contact   Carol A. Burns, Director
Internship Program
Southern Illinois University Press
P.O. Box 3697
Carbondale, IL 62901
618-453-6628; fax 618-453-1221

Stanford Alumni Association
Stanford, California

STANFORD PROFESSIONAL PUBLISHING COURSE

Level
Professional

Program Objective
Thirteen-day course on book and magazine publishing designed to provide developmental training for mid- to upper-level book or magazine publishing professionals. Course presented by industry leaders.

Program Description
Course presented in a series of seminars and case studies. Topics include editing, design, production, marketing, sales, advertising, finance, new technologies, and publishing law. Classes meet weekdays, evenings, weekends during the summer. Job placement services available on ad hoc basis only.

Admission
Admission selective. In 1991, 250 applied, 165 were accepted, 165 enrolled. Requires application and statement of expectations.

Faculty
Mikkel Aaland, photographer and coprincipal, Tor Productions; James Adams, professor of engineering, Stanford University; David Armario, art director and design consultant; Lawrence P. Ashmead, executive editor, HarperCollins; Jim Autry, president/magazine publishing group, Meredith Corporation; Robert Baensch, senior vice president/marketing, Rizzoli International Publications, Inc.; Alice Bandy, president, Bandy Direct Marketing; Grant Barnes, director, Stanford University Press; Walter Bernard, partner, WBMG; Simon Michael Bessie, publisher, Cornelia & Michael Bessie Books; David Brown, president, The Manhattan Project; Russell Brown, art director, Adobe Systems, Inc.; Rosalie Bruno, president, Circulation Specialists, Inc.; Robert Burgelman, associate professor/management, Stanford University; John Mack Carter, editor-in-chief, *Good Housekeeping;* Ani Charmichean, director/national trade markets, Harper San Francisco; George Clark; director/single copy sales, International Data Group West; Ken Coburn, president, Interprint; Gregory Curtis, editor, *Texas Monthly;* Andrew Danish, design director, *Stanford Magazine;* Sandra Dijkstra, president, Sandra Dijkstra Literary Agency; Ann Dilworth, president/general and international publishing group, Addison-Wesley; Henrik Drescher, illustrator; Sally Elliot, president, Benjamin/Cummings Publishing Co.; Michela English, senior vice president, National Geographic Society; Pamela Fiori, editorial director, American Express Publishing; Brendan Gill, columnist, *The New Yorker;* Erwin Glikes, president and publisher, The Free Press; David Godine, president, David Godine Publishers, Inc.; George Green, president, Hearst Magazines International; Carole Hall, executive editor, Touchstone Books/Simon & Schuster; Joseph Hanson, president, Hanson Publishing Group; Dale Harris, director/center for telecommunications, Stanford University; Katherine Head, vice president/production, Wadsworth Publishing Co.; Duvall Hecht, president, Books on Tape; Nigel Holmes, graphics director, *Time;* Ivan Inerfeld, partner, Coopers & Lybrand; Carol Janeway, vice president and senior editor, Alfred A. Knopf, Inc.; Dorothy Kalins, editor-in-chief, *Metropolitan Home;* John Klingel, vice president/marketing, Time Publishing Ventures, Inc.; Laura Lamar, partner, MAX; Martin Levin, counsellor to publishers, Cowan, Liebowitz, & Latman; Ellen Levine, editor-in-chief, *Redbook;* Ed Lewis, publish-

er and chief executive, *Essence;* Dayna Macy, publicity and marketing director, Earthworks Press; Walter Mathews, president, Walter Mathews Associates, Inc.; Peter Mayer, chairman and CEO, Penguin USA; Gianfranco Monacelli, president, CEO, and publisher, Rizzoli International Publications, Inc.; Henry Muller, managing editor, *Time;* Dian-Aziza Ooka, art director, *Parenting;* Jane Palecek, art director, *In Health;* John Papanek, managing editor, *Sports Illustrated;* Maynard Parker, editor, *Newsweek;* George Peterson, director/educational media, National Geographic Society; Phil Pfeffer, chairman of the board and CEO, Ingram Distribution Group; Bernice Randall, president, Bernice Randall & Associates; Steve Rees, magazine management consultant; Michael Rogers, coprincipal, Tor Productions, and senior editor, *Newsweek;* Stephen Roxburgh, vice president and publisher, Books for Young Readers, Farrar, Straus & Giroux; Thomas O. Ryder, president, American Express Publishing Corporation; Paul Saffo, research fellow, Institute for the Future; Eric Schrier, editor, *In Health;* Charles Selden, president, fp Video Services; Brian Smale, photographer; Rick Smolan, photographer and publisher, *Against All Odds;* James Stockton, president and art director, James Stockton & Associates; Richard B. Stolley, editorial director, Time, Inc., Magazines; D. J. Stout, art director, *Texas Monthly;* Tom Suzuki, president and art director, Tom Suzuki Design; Nan A. Talese, senior vice president, Doubleday, and president, publisher, and editorial director, Nan A. Talese Books; Scott F. Turow, author; Mark Ulriksen, art director, *Focus;* Alberto Vitale, president and CEO, Random House, Inc.; John Warnock, president and CEO, Adobe Systems; George Young, Ten Speed Press.

Expenses and Accommodations
$2,800 tuition. $35 application fee. Other expenses include housing (on-campus housing approximately $300 for two-week period) and meals.

Contact   William Merz, Course Manager
Stanford Professional Publishing Course
Bowman Alumni House
Stanford, CA 94305
415-725-1083; fax 415-725-8676

State University of New York at Albany
Albany, New York

CONTEMPORARY PUBLISHING

Sponsor
School of Information Science and Policy, Nelson A. Rockefeller College of Public Affairs and Policy

Level
Graduate

Course Objective
Designed to introduce students to the structure of the publishing industry and publishing houses and to book distribution systems. Aimed primarily at students preparing for careers in libraries and other information agencies, but open to students interested in careers in publishing.

Course Description
Topics include nature and structure of the publishing industry, structure of publishing houses, printing and production processes, editorial work, author/publisher relations, marketing and distribution systems, publisher/library relations, and international aspects of publishing. Course is part of the M.L.S or M.S. in information science curriculum. Meets weekdays; students typically take three semesters to complete the M.L.S. program and four to complete the M.S. program. Job placement available for librarian/information science positions only.

Admission
Admission selective. Requires application, essay, letters of reference, college transcript, undergraduate degree.

Faculty
Philip B. Eppard, assistant professor.

Expenses and Accommodations
$402 per course (state residents); $822 per course (nonresidents). $35 application fee. Other expenses include $1,300–$1,700 per semester for housing, $60 for books. Housing available.

Contact   Philip B. Eppard, Assistant Professor
School of Information Science and Policy
135 Western Avenue
Draper 113
State University of New York
Albany, NY 12222
518-442-5110; fax 518-442-5232

State University of New York at Buffalo
Buffalo, New York

INTERNATIONAL PUBLISHING AND THE DISTRIBUTION OF KNOWLEDGE

Sponsors
School of Information and Library Studies and the Graduate School of Education, Administration, and Policy

Level
Graduate

Course Objective
Designed to provide graduate students matriculated in either the M.L.S. program or the department of education with a general background in publishing books and journals and an analysis of the distribution of knowledge worldwide.

Course Description
The 3-credit graduate course covers the role of books and journals in the modern world, international knowledge networks, how books are produced, copyright, comparative aspects of scholarly publishing, the role and function of journals in knowledge distribution, third-world publishing, and the library and the knowledge process. Course meets evenings, one semester. Job placement services available.

Admission
Admission to master's program selective. For spring/fall 1991, 152 applied, 115 were accepted, 85 enrolled in the M.L.S. program. Acceptance to the School of Information and Library Studies requires application, essay, three letters of reference, college transcript, undergraduate degree (international students must submit Graduate Record Examination and Test of English as a Foreign Language scores and a financial statement). Interview recommended.

Faculty
Philip G. Altbach, professor, Department of Education, Administration, and Policy.

Expenses and Accommodations
$134 per credit (state residents); $274 per credit (nonresidents). $35 M.L.S. program application fee. Approximately $30 university fees. Housing available.

Contact   Philip G. Altbach, Professor
Department of Education, Administration, and Policy
468 Baldy Hall
State University of New York
Buffalo, NY 16240
716-636-2487

Syracuse University
Syracuse, New York

BACHELOR OF SCIENCE IN MAGAZINE

Sponsor
S. I. Newhouse School of Public Communications

Level
Undergraduate/Graduate

Program Objective
To give students the opportunity to perfect writing and editing skills; the practical skills needed to handle problems in layout, photography, and research; and an understanding of communication theory and ethics.

Program Description
Major course requirements include Communication and Society, Communications Law and Ethics, Introduction to the Graphic Arts, Introduction to the Magazine, Magazine Article Writing, Magazine Editing, News Writing, and Reporting. Electives may be chosen from the magazine, photography, graphics, advertising, and public relations areas. Completion of course work leads to B.S. in magazine. Classes meet weekdays; students typically take four years to complete their degree. Includes internships and special projects. Job placement services available.

Admission
Requires students be enrolled at the university. Admission selective. Enrollment figures N/A.

Faculty
William Galvin, professor and chairman, Magazine Department; J. T. W. Hubbard, professor, Magazine Department; Alfred Balk, associate professor, Magazine Department.

Expenses and Accommodations
$19,547 per year for tuition, room, and board. $40 application fee. $220 health fee, $98 activity fee, and approximately $550 for books and supplies. Housing available.

Contact   William Galvin, Chairman
Magazine Department
215 University Place
Syracuse University
Syracuse, NY 13244
315-443-9246

Texas Writers Association
Dallas, Texas

NATIONAL MAGAZINE EDITORS CONFERENCE

Sponsor
Conference/Seminar Department

Level
Professional

Program Objective
Designed to meet the needs of experienced professional magazine writers and new editors who are trying to break into the magazine market. Reviews basic skills and promotes understanding of individual magazine editorial needs.

Program Description
Topics of intensive two-day workshops include What the Editors Want, Think Like an Editor, Researching the Article, Getting the Interview, Query Letter, On Writing Well, Electronic Submission, Finding the Articles, How to Interview Anyone, Photos, and Round-up Articles. Meets on a weekend. Job placement services not available.

Admission
Admission open. In 1991, 140 enrolled. Requires application.

Faculty
Faculty consists of editors of major national magazines, including *Field and Stream, Personal Computing, Popular Science, Lear's, Art and Antiques, MS, Travel Holiday, Vista, Essense, Emerge, American Health, Playboy, Parade,* and *Better Homes and Gardens.*

Expenses and Accommodations
$250 members; $400 nonmembers. Other expenses include accommodations and transportation.

Contact   Jheri Fleet, Executive Director
Texas Writers Association
219 Preston Royal Shopping Center
Suite #3
Dallas, TX 75230
214-363-9979

U.S. Department of Agriculture Graduate School
Washington, D.C.

COURSES AND CERTIFICATES OF ACCOMPLISHMENT IN EDITING, DESKTOP PUBLISHING, PUBLICATION MANAGEMENT, AND PHOTOGRAPHY

Level
Professional

Program Objective
Designed to offer career-related training to adults, regardless of level of education or employment. Courses in the editing, publishing, and design fields are designed for beginners and experienced employees.

Program Description
Courses are available in different formats: home-study correspondence courses, evening courses offered on a quarterly system, and short weekday training courses. The school is not a degree-granting institution. It offers certificates of accomplishment, and many of its courses have received credit recommendations from the American Council on Education's Program on Noncollegiate Sponsored Instruction to facilitate transfer to degree programs.

Admission
Admission open. Students register to take courses as required. Some courses have prerequisites. Requires students to be at least 18 years old; registration necessary. Prior experience may be recommended in course description.

Faculty
The school employs nearly 800 part-time faculty members who have backgrounds in government or higher education.

Expenses and Accommodations
$164–$300 per course. Other expenses include books and materials. Housing not available.

Contact   Information Office
USDA Graduate School
600 Maryland Avenue, SW
Room 129
Washington, DC 20024
202-447-4419; fax 202-382-8632

University of Alabama
Tuscaloosa, Alabama

FUNDAMENTALS OF MAGAZINE PUBLISHING

Sponsor
Journalism Department, College of Communication

Level
Undergraduate/Graduate/Professional

Course Objective
This seminar course is designed to provide a basic understanding of book publishing in the U.S. and in a global context. It will help students understand how book publishing companies exist in a competitive market and the important social role of the medium.

Course Description
Students are expected to read each issue of *Publisher's Weekly* cover to cover (subscriptions will be provided) for class discussion and assignments; prepare and present a book review; write a paper on a topical issue affecting book publishing; profile a book publishing house; keep a journal. Course results in 3 credit hours toward the bachelor's or master's degree. Meets weekdays, evenings, weekends for a single semester. Includes field trips, internships, and special projects. Job placement services available.

Admission
Admission to the seminar open to all students enrolled at the university. In academic year 1990–91, 6 enrolled. Admission to the university requires application, interview, high school transcript, college transcript.

Faculty
George Grangoulis, associate professor.

Expenses and Accommodations
$968 per semester (state resident); $2,400 per semester (nonresident). Housing available.

Contact   Dr. Ed Mullins, Dean
College of Communication
P.O. Box 870172
University of Alabama
Tuscaloosa, AL 35487-0172
205-348-5520; fax 205-348-6213

University of Alabama
Tuscaloosa, Alabama

MASTER OF FINE ARTS PROGRAM IN THE BOOK ARTS

Sponsor
School of Library and Information Studies

Level
Graduate

Program Objective
Designed to instruct students in the craft of making books by hand, including bookbinding, papermaking, and printing. The orientation is to make books with literary content high in craft values.

Program Description
Includes four classes in both bookbinding and letterpress printing and Making Paper by Hand, History of the Book, Modern Book Publishing, Decorated Papers, and Edition Bookbinding. Program awards M.F.A. in the book arts. Forty-eight credit hours required to complete program. Classes meet weekdays; students typically take four semesters to complete program. Includes field trips, internships, and special projects. Job placement services available.

Admission
Admission selective. In 1990, 12 applied, 8 were accepted, 6 enrolled. Requires application, letters of reference, college transcript, undergraduate degree, and a high level of motivation. Interview recommended.

Faculty
Paula Marie Gourley, assistant professor/bookbinding teacher; Steve Miller, associate professor/ printing, papermaking; G. Barry Neavill, associate professor/History of the Book.

Expenses and Accommodations
$905 per semester (state residents); $2,243 per semester (nonresidents). $20 application fee. Housing available.

Contact   Steve Miller, Coordinator
                M.F.A. Program in the Book Arts
                Box 870252
                University of Alabama
                Tuscaloosa, AL 35487-0252
                205-348-1525; fax 205-348-3746

University of California at Berkeley
Berkeley, California

CERTIFICATE PROGRAM IN BOOK AND MAGAZINE PUBLISHING

Sponsor
Berkeley Extension, Business and Management Department

Level
Professional

Program Objective
Designed to meet the needs of people who want to enter the field of publishing or who want to increase their skills in the major areas of publishing. The program focuses on the business aspects of publishing in the areas of editorial, production, marketing, and finance. Students have the option to choose the book or magazine track.

Program Description
Courses include Working as an Editor in the Book Business; Business and Financial Aspects of Publishing; Contemporary Issues in Publishing: Traditional Functions and Computer Techniques; Principles of Manufacturing and Production Management; Marketing in the Book Business; Marketing in the Magazine Business; and Working as an Editor in the Magazine Business. The program requires completion of seven courses (225 semester hours). Classes meet evenings; students typically take four semesters to complete program. Job placement services not available.

Admission
Admission open. In calendar year 1990, 30 applied, 30 were accepted, 30 enrolled. Requires application, bachelor's degree.

Faculty
Faculty changes from year to year. All are professionals in publishing.

Expenses and Accommodations
$230–$250 per course. $60 application fee. Housing not available.

Contact   Richard J. Caramella, Continuing Education Specialist
Business and Management Department
UC Berkeley Extension
2223 Fulton Street
Berkeley, CA 94720
510-642-4231; fax 510-643-8683

University of Chicago
Chicago, Illinois

UNIVERSITY OF CHICAGO PUBLISHING PROGRAM

Sponsor
Office of Continuing Education

Level
Professional

Program Objective
Developed by the staff of the University of Chicago Press. Designed to offer ongoing professional development to publishing professionals in the form of quarter-long courses, seminars, and one-day workshops, and to provide a yearlong introduction to the field for beginners. The yearlong introduction may be followed by a second year, during which participants may specialize in a particular area of publishing.

Program Description
Courses and seminars include Introduction to Free-lance Writing; Basic Manuscript Editing; Professional Free-lance Writing; Advanced Manuscript Editing; The Art and Craft of Writing Fiction; Marketing Your Article and Yourself; Computerized Manuscript Processing; Electronic Manuscripts and the Publishing Firm; Marketing Your Nonfiction Book and Yourself; Introduction to Publication Design; Introduction to Indexing; Essentials of Publication Design; Entrancing Young Children: The Art of Writing Picture Books; Medical Editing; Introduction to Magazine Production; Introduction to Book Production; Copyright Issues in Publishing; Essentials of Design for the Editor; Management Development for Publishing Professionals; and How to Create and Use Photography in Publications. Participants may enroll in a seminar or single class or sign up for the yearlong sequence. Certificates are presented for every class successfully completed. Students who complete a first- or second-year series receive a diploma for each year's work, acknowledging their completion of the program. Classes and seminars meet weekdays, evenings, weekends; students typically take six trimesters to complete the two yearlong sequences. Some courses require students to submit samples of their work. Job placement services not available.

Admission
Admission open. Recommends undergraduate degree.

Faculty
Faculty changes from year to year, largely composed of staff from the University of Chicago Press.

Expenses and Accommodations
$285 per course; $795 per yearlong sequence (three courses). Housing available.

Contact   Stephanie Medlock, Director
Publishing Program
University of Chicago
5835 S. Kimbark Avenue
Room 207
Chicago, IL 60637
312-702-1682; fax 312-702-6814

University of Connecticut
Storrs, Connecticut

THE REALITIES OF PUBLISHING

Sponsor
Department of English

Level
Undergraduate

Course Objective
This stand-alone course is designed for English majors who are interested in pursuing careers in writing and/or publishing.

Course Description
Half of the course is devoted to magazine publishing—writing, production, economics, public relations, and advertising—and half to book publishing, including trade, text, and reference books. Other topics include literacy, censorship, conglomerate control, reviews, methods of distribution, and the small-press movement. Class meets weekdays. Includes internships and special projects. Job placement services not available.

Admission
Admission to the course is open on a space-available basis to all undergraduate English majors. Admission for internships is selective. Internship requires application, essay, interview, college transcript.

Faculty
Feenie Ziner, associate professor, English; William Sheidley, professor, English.

Expenses and Accommodations
$1,890 tuition, $153 per credit (state residents); $6,690 tuition, $353 per credit (nonresidents). Other expenses include fees, room and board, course materials. Housing available.

Contact   Feenie Ziner, Associate Professor
Department of English, U-25
University of Connecticut
Storrs, CT 06269
203-486-2282

University of Denver
Denver, Colorado

UNIVERSITY OF DENVER PUBLISHING INSTITUTE

Sponsor
Division of Arts, Humanities and Social Sciences

Level
Graduate/Professional

Program Objective
Designed for college graduates who are interested in careers in book publishing, for career changers, and for people already employed in publishing or related fields who want a broad overview of the industry as a whole and knowledge of editing, marketing, and production techniques.

Program Description
Courses include workshops on editing, marketing, and production; lecture/teaching sessions on editor/author/agent relations, university press/scholarly publishing, college/primary-secondary textbooks, children's books, paperback publishing, international publishing, subsidiary rights, book clubs, publicity/promotion, economics/financial aspects of publishing, small presses, reference books, role of the sales rep, wholesale and retail bookselling; and special sessions on career planning. Completion of program can result in 6 quarter-hours of graduate credit and a certificate of completion signed by the university provost, the director of the institute, and the university dean. Requires completion of forty-six half-day sessions over four weeks during the summer. Classes meet weekdays. Students must complete the following assignments before beginning the program: read and evaluate a raw manuscript for editing workshop, read a set of bound galleys of an about-to-be-published trade book, write a publicity release, and complete assignments for reference books and production. Includes field trips and special projects. Job placement services available.

Admission
Admission selective. In the academic year 1990–91, 150 applied, 100 were accepted, 90 enrolled. Requires application, essay, letters of reference, college transcript, undergraduate degree (occasionally accepts students with publishing experience and no degree).

Faculty
Over 50 publishing executives make up the faculty each year. Faculty members include Arnold Dolin, vice president/associate publisher, New American Library; Marvin Brown, CEO, Penguin USA; Robert Baensch, senior vice president, Rizzoli Publishing Co.; Richard Greenberg, president, Wadsworth Publishing Co.; Richard Hunt, director/marketing, Bantam Doubleday Dell; Virginia Barber, president, Barber Literary Agency; Barbara Grossman, publisher, Charles Scribner's Sons; Czeslaw Jan Grycz, director/technology study project, University of California; Erwin Glikes, president, The Free Press/Macmillan; Susan Hirschman, senior vice president, Greenwillow Books.

Expenses and Accommodations
$2,000 for entire program. $35 application fee. Estimated additional expenses include $800 for room and board. Housing available.

Contact   Director
University of Denver Publishing Institute
2075 South University Boulevard
#D-114
University of Denver
Denver, CO 80210
303-871-2570; fax 303-871-2501

University of Illinois at Urbana-Champaign
Urbana, Illinois

CONTEMPORARY BOOK PUBLISHING

Sponsor
Graduate School of Library and Information Science

Level
Graduate

Course Objective
Designed to describe the world of publishing for students preparing for careers in librarianship.

Course Description
Surveys twentieth-century book publishing, placing it in an economic, social, and literary context, and emphasizes its economic structure, author/publisher relationships, promotion, distribution, and the influence of the industry on librarianship. Completion of the course may be used as an elective toward an M.S. in library and information science. Course meets weekdays; students typically take three semesters to complete M.S. program. Students must complete Foundations of Library and Information Science as a prerequisite. Job placement services available.

Admission
Admission open to those enrolled in the M.S. program. Enrollment figures N/A. Admission to the M.S. program requires application, essay, letters of reference, college transcript, undergraduate degree, and Graduate Record Examinations scores.

Faculty
Faculty members for the course are either adjunct or visiting professors.

Expenses and Accommodations
$1,838 tuition and fees per semester (state residents); $4,314 (nonresidents). Housing available.

Contact   Curt McKay, Assistant to the Dean
Graduate School of Library and Information Science
410 David Kinley Hall
1407 W. Gregory
University of Illinois
Urbana, IL 61801
217-333-3280; fax 217-244-3302

University of Pittsburgh
Pittsburgh, Pennsylvania

MASTER OF LIBRARY SCIENCE

Sponsor
School of Library and Information Science

Level
Graduate

Program Objective
Designed to educate information professionals interested in general issues affecting publishers and publishing.

Program Description
Classes include Resources for Children, Resources for Young Adults, Resources and Services for Adults, Government Information Resources and Services, African-American Resources and Services, Social Sciences Resources and Services, Science and Technology Resources and Services, Business and Economics Resources and Services, Latin-American Resources and Services, History of Books, Printing and Publishing, Interactive Graphics, Document Processing. Completion of program leads to M.S. in library science. Requires completion of twelve courses. Classes meet weekdays, evenings, weekends; students typically take three trimesters to complete program. Includes field trips, internships, and special projects. Job placement services available.

Admission
Admission selective. In the academic year 1990–91, 158 applied, 138 were accepted, 69 enrolled. Requires application, essay, letters of reference, college transcript, undergraduate degree.

Faculty
Stephen Almagno, professor; Mary K. Biagini, associate professor; Ellen Detlefsen, associate professor; E. J. Josey, professor; Margaret Kimmel, professor; Richard Krzys, professor; Michael Spring, assistant professor; Chris Tomer, assistant professor; Blanche Woolls, professor.

Expenses and Accommodations
$3,070 tuition per semester (state residents); $6,140 (nonresidents). $30 application fee for U.S. students; $40 application fee for international students. Other fees estimated at $160. Housing not available.

Contact   Admissions Coordinator
School of Library and Information Science
505 SLIS Building
University of Pittsburgh
Pittsburgh, PA 15260
412-624-5230; fax 412-624-5231

University of the Arts, Philadelphia College of Art and Design
Philadelphia, Pennsylvania

MASTER OF FINE ARTS, BOOK ARTS/PRINTMAKING

Sponsor
Printmaking Department

Level
Graduate

Program Objective
Designed to advance students' conceptual abilities while developing technical skills in traditional and state-of-the-art processes and to prepare them for careers in academia or professional endeavors.

Program Description
Course topics include book design, typography/letterpress, offset lithography, bookbinding, drawing workshop, history of the book, book arts printmaking colloquium, university seminar, thesis studio, humanities electives, and studio electives. Completion of 60 credits leads to M.F.A. Classes meet weekdays; students typically take four semesters to complete program. Includes field trips. Job placement services available.

Admission
Admission selective. In the academic year 1990–91, 27 applied, 7 were accepted, 7 enrolled. Requires application, essay, letters of reference, high school transcript, college transcript, undergraduate degree, portfolio review (by submission of slides). Interview recommended.

Faculty
Frank Galuszka, professor; James Green, lecturer and curator of printed books at the Library Company of Philadelphia; Lois M. Johnson, professor; Nathan Knobler, professor; Hedi Kyle, lecturer and conservator at the American Philosophical Society; Mary Phelan, assistant professor; Patricia M. Smith, assistant professor; David Tafler, associate professor; Susan Viguers, associate professor.

Expenses and Accommodations
$10,295 per year. $30 application fee. Other expenses include course supplies. Housing not available.

Contact   Mary Phelan, Director
University of the Arts
Broad and Pine Streets
Philadelphia, PA 19102
215-875-1119; fax 215-875-5467

Indexes

Geographical Index

Subject Index

Book and Magazine Publishing (General)

Books, Children's

INTERNSHIPS 1992

Describing over 50,000 opportunities, this is the most complete annual directory available for college students and career-changers seeking on-the-job training positions.

Thousands of college students and adults changing careers or reentering the work force turn to *Internships* every year to find temporary jobs that will open doors to full-time work. This edition lists over 50,000 positions in some two dozen career fields in:

- Communications
- Creative arts
- Human services
- International business
- Public affairs
- Science/industry

Complete details on the position, desired qualifications, compensation, whom to contact, and more are included.

$27.95 paperback

JOBS FOR ENGLISH MAJORS AND OTHER SMART PEOPLE

Updated for the 1990s, this book shows job hunters how to use creative techniques that increase their chances of success in today's changing job market. Specific pointers include:

- How to write resumes and cover letters that stand out
- How to uncover—and seize—hidden opportunities
- How to use information interviews
- How to do research that can lead to a job

This book will be of real value to *anyone* with a college degree—not just a liberal arts graduate—who's looking for a job.

$11.95 paperback

THE 90-MINUTE RESUME
For First-Time Resume Writers

THE ADVANCED 90-MINUTE RESUME
For Resume Revisers

The 90-Minute Resume: For First-Time Resume Writers covers the basics that every resume-writer should know, from choosing a format to effectively describing accomplishments (even when they *seem* insignificant) to getting the resume into the right hands. Its companion, *The Advanced 90-Minute Resume: For Resume Revisers,* features guidance on changing an existing resume from adequate to dynamite. Whether you're a job-hunting novice or veteran, these books will give you excellent resume guidance.

Available May 1992

$7.95 each paperback

Peterson's Annual Guides to Graduate Study
Complete Coverage of More Than 31,000 Graduate and Professional Programs in the U.S. and Canada

PETERSON'S GUIDE TO GRADUATE AND PROFESSIONAL PROGRAMS: AN OVERVIEW 1992

$21.95 paperback

PETERSON'S GUIDE TO GRADUATE PROGRAMS IN THE HUMANITIES AND SOCIAL SCIENCES 1992

$33.95 paperback

PETERSON'S GUIDE TO GRADUATE PROGRAMS IN THE BIOLOGICAL AND AGRICULTURAL SCIENCES 1992

$39.95 paperback

PETERSON'S GUIDE TO GRADUATE PROGRAMS IN BUSINESS, EDUCATION, HEALTH, AND LAW 1992

$21.95 paperback

PETERSON'S GUIDE TO GRADUATE PROGRAMS IN THE PHYSICAL SCIENCES AND MATHEMATICS 1992

$29.95 paperback

PETERSON'S GUIDE TO GRADUATE PROGRAMS IN ENGINEERING AND APPLIED SCIENCES 1992

$33.95 paperback

Look for these and other Peterson's titles in your local bookstore